RECEIVED
2 7 FEB 2012

on Morrell Site

KT-568-868

812
CAR
(D23)

The BIG Book of Customer Service Training Games

Quick, Fun Activities for all Customer Facing Employees

Peggy Carlaw

Vasudha Kathleen Deming

WITHDRAWN
COLLEGE
LIBRARY

McGraw-Hill

New York   San Francisco   Washington, D.C.   Auckland   Bogotá
Caracas   Lisbon   London   Madrid   Mexico City   Milan
Montreal   New Delhi   San Juan   Singapore
Sydney   Tokyo   Toronto

Warwickshire College

00675652

The Big Book of Customer Service Training Games
Quick, Fun Activities for all Customer Facing Employees

Peggy Carlaw, Vasudha Kathleen Deming

WARWICKSHIRE COLLEGE
LIBRARY

Class No
658.812

Acc No
00675652

Price & Loan Type
£14.99

ISBN: 0077114760

 **Professional**

Published by:
McGraw-Hill Publishing Company
Shoppenhangers Road, Maidenhead, Berkshire, England, SL6 2QL
Telephone: 44 (0) 1628 502500
Fax: 44 (0) 1628 770224
Website: www.mcgraw-hill.co.uk

British Library Cataloguing in Publication Data
A catalogue record of this book is available from the British Library.

Library of Congress Cataloging Number: 98-067041

McGraw-Hill books are available at special quantity discounts. Please contact
the corporate sales executive.

Copyright © 1999 by The McGraw-Hill Companies, Inc. All rights reserved.
Printed in the United States of America. Except as permitted under the United
States Copyright Act of 1976, no part of this publication may be reproduced or
distributed in any form or by any means, or stored in a database or retrieval
system, without the prior written permission of the publisher.

Reprinted 2007

Printed in Great Britain by Bell and Bain Ltd., Glasgow

Mixed Sources
Product group from well-managed
forests and other controlled sources
www.fsc.org Cert no. TT-COC-002769
© 1996 Forest Stewardship Council

The **McGraw·Hill** Companies

Contents

First Impressions   73

Participants examine their own biases and impressions based on the appearance of people in pictures, then discuss what impressions customers might have of them, based on their appearance.

You Look Marvelous!   75

Participants review pictures to determine the importance of posture and appearance in adding meaning to communication.

Face Off   79

Some participants demonstrate facial expressions while other participants guess which emotion is being demonstrated.

Five Pillars of Success   83

Participants identify five basic communication skills that are essential to success in face-to-face customer service.

Chapter 5.   Make It a Great Day   87
Games for Establishing Rapport with Every Customer

Hidden Rapport   89

Participants work together on a puzzle to uncover a variety of techniques for building rapport with customers.

I Feel for You   93

Participants work in pairs to rewrite dry, rote statements to show more empathy for customers.

Accentuate the Positive   99

Participants learn to let customers know how they will benefit from the way their requests and needs are handled.

And How's the Weather?   103

Participants learn to pick up clues from customers that can help them to build a strong rapport by studying pictures of "customers" and coming up with statements they might use to make pleasant, light conversation.

Chapter 10. What About Us?   191
Games for Improving Service to Your Internal Customers

Acknowledgments

I'd like to thank Dick Roe for bringing me into the field of training and for being such a great boss and mentor. I'd also like to thank Richard Narramore—long a friend and now an editor—for his vision, expertise, and support during the completion of this book.

Vasudha Kathleen Deming

And I'd like to thank our customers for their belief in our programs and for allowing us to work with them to develop new ways of excelling in the level of service they provide.

Peggy Carlaw

Introduction

The most important relationship your company has is the one between your customers and the employees they interact with either in person or on the phone. Whether you're a trainer, manager, or supervisor, anything you can do to strengthen that relationship will ultimately benefit your organization in a number of ways.

We believe that customer service can be—ought to be—an intrinsically rewarding profession. There's just something about serving people that's immensely satisfying to the human psyche—even if that service consists of taking an order, giving out information, or selling a pair of shoes. It's in this vein that we've created this volume of customer service games.

The games are fun, motivational activities centered around skill learning and skill use. They build confidence, lift morale, spark enthusiasm, stimulate creativity, and ultimately achieve results in the real-time customer service environment. We've consistently found that employees look forward to these games and become fully immersed while playing. You may be surprised which members of your department come to life when game time arrives!

The games are designed to be administered by anyone who manages, supervises, or trains customer service personnel. And they're meant to be played by anyone who has a customer: customer service reps, sales reps, telemarketers, technical support reps, field technicians, cashiers, hospitality staff, etc.

Some of the games are quick, fun energizers that serve to raise participants' awareness of customer service issues. Others are full-scale activities that teach a skill and offer participants the opportunity to practice the skill in an informal, nonthreatening environment. There are any number of ways you can use the games: as stand-alone training activities, as warm-ups to a more intensive training session, or in combination with one another to constitute a comprehensive customer service training event.

Alternatively, you can use these ten- to twenty-minute games at your staff meetings, Friday afternoon discussion groups, brown bag lunches, and anywhere else you see fit. You don't even have to tell participants it's "training!"

The games will not only teach your employees to do their jobs better but will also inspire them to offer a level of service that brings new meaning and motivation to their jobs. In turn, this customer service excellence will help to set your company apart from—and above—the rest.

> "Choose to serve.
> The world will start loving you
> Immediately."
> —*Sri Chinmoy*

How to Use This Book

The book contains 50 games—long and short, simple and complex—that address ten different categories of customer service. We've endeavored to make the games straightforward and easy to deliver. Following is our advice to you for getting the most out of this book and out of your customer service employees.

Tips for Success

- Prepare for your training session by taking the time to thoroughly review each game beforehand. The better you understand the objective, flow, and tone of each game, the more successful the training will be.

- Keep in mind that these are *games*. If you maintain a playful, enthusiastic approach, you'll find that the participants too will feel comfortable and motivated to play.

- Whenever possible, bring in some real-life examples of problems and situations you've observed at your organization. This will help participants to transfer the learning to their on-the-job environment.

- Play the role of facilitator rather than teacher. The most effective learning comes when you *guide* the participants and *they* make the discovery.

- Adapt the games to the climate and culture in which your employees work. If they respond well to rewards, then offer candy, gift certificates, or other small rewards at the conclusion of each game. If your employees can be trusted to have fun-spirited competitions (as opposed to heated battles), then go ahead and turn the games into competitions. Each group can choose a team name and can show their team spirit by clapping, cheering, etc.

- Except for a few props, we've given you everything you need to successfully facilitate the games. Nevertheless, we encourage you to be creative in expanding upon the games in any way that will make them meaningful for the participants.

- All the games lend themselves to further discussion and review. Follow up on what participants learned by debriefing the game, creating job aids, or establishing a game plan for ongoing practice and review.

It's Who You Are

Games for Developing a Customer-Focused Attitude

Customer Service Means . . .

In a Nutshell

Participants work in groups to piece together several definitions of service (provided on pre-cut pages). The objective is to help participants understand the meaning of serving customers. This game is particularly useful for new employees or as a lead-in to developing a definition of customer service for your own department.

Time

10–15 minutes.

What You'll Need

One copy of the service definition sheet on page 6 and one envelope for each three participants.

What to Do

Divide participants into groups of three or four. Give each group an envelope containing the contents of the hand-out. Write, "Customer service means . . ." on a blank flip-chart or white board.

Explain that in the envelope are phrases that, when assembled, provide seven definitions of service. Their job is to work together as a team to assemble the phrases in a way that completes the sentence, "Customer service means . . ." Each phrase must be a complete, logical sentence. They must use all the pieces and each piece can be used only once.

Mix non-native English speakers with native English speakers to avoid syntax errors. If the groups are slow to get started, advise them to start each phrase with a verb such as "finding."

After five minutes, have each team read its definitions out loud.

Answers

Customer service means:
- Doing ordinary things extraordinarily well.
- Going beyond what's expected.
- Adding value and integrity to every interaction.
- Being at your best with every customer.
- Discovering new ways to delight those you serve.
- Surprising yourself with how much you can do.
- Taking care of the customer like you would take care of your grandmother.

Discussion Questions

Q: Are all these definitions true?

A: *Be prepared for class answers to differ.*

Q: Which definition do you like best?

A: *Field answers.*

Q: Why isn't there one common definition?

A: *Because customer service means different things to different people. Notice, though, that all these definitions talk about putting energy and enthusiasm into your interactions with customers.*

If You Have More Time

Ask participants for their definitions of customer service. List words and phrases on a flip-chart. Develop into a definition of customer service for your department.

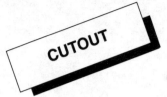

Customer Service Means . . .

Instructions:

Photocopy one sheet for every three participants (card stock works best if you have it on hand). Cut out the words and phrases by following the dotted lines. Put each set of cut-up words and phrases in its own envelope. Each envelope should contain the words on this sheet (24 pieces in all) and there should be one envelope for each group of three participants.

✂

doing	ordinary things	extraordinarily well
going	beyond	what's expected
adding	value and integrity	to every interaction
being	at your best	with every customer
discovering	new ways	to delight	those you serve
surprising	yourself	with how much	you can do
taking care	of the customer	like you would
take care of your grandmother

Tip! If you'll be playing this game again, you might want to print each set on different colored card stock. After the game is over, have participants count to be sure there are 24 pieces, then put them back in the envelope. You'll be all set for next time!

Mission Possible

In a Nutshell

In this activity, participants work together to create a mission statement for their department. This is an ideal activity for injecting a new level of enthusiasm into the department and bringing a new sense of meaning to work.

Time

20–25 minutes.

What You'll Need

Copies of your corporate mission statement, if you have one, or copies of other companies' mission statements that you find inspiring. Blank flip-chart paper and marker pens (one for each three to five participants).

What to Do

Discuss the concept of a mission statement. Hand out your corporate mission statement (or those from other companies if you don't have one).

Put participants into groups of three to five and give each group a piece of flip-chart paper and a marker pen. Explain that their job will be to work together to come up with a brief mission statement for their department.

Review the overhead on page 9 and tell participants to discuss the answers to their questions before beginning to write their mission statement.

Allow 15 minutes for this part of the activity. If there is more than one group, ask each group to select a spokesperson to present its mission statement to the class.

Listen to the mission statements and discuss as needed. Be sure the mission statements do not contradict your company mission statement.

If there is more than one group, ask each group to appoint one member to represent them on a committee to finalize the mission statement. Suggest that the committee meet at lunch or arrange for them to have time off during work to finalize the statement over the course of the next week. When the mission statement is complete, obtain the finalized mission statement and print a nice copy to be posted in the department's work area. Also consider printing smaller copies for each participant to post in his or her work area. If possible, bring the participants together again to present the final mission statement.

If You Have More Time

Have each participant write a personal mission statement that complements the statement written by the department. Give them nice paper so that they can print the statements and post them at their desks.

Defining Your Mission

- **Why do customers remember us?**

- **How do customers feel after they deal with us?**

- **What do customers tell their friends about us?**

- **In what ways do we help one another in our department?**

- **How does our department support the general aim of our company?**

Assets and Opportunities

In a Nutshell

In this activity, participants review skills that are essential to the customer service role, assess their own competence in each skill, and develop an action plan for improving their proficiency. This activity helps new employees understand the assets possessed by top-notch customer service representatives and gives all employees an opportunity to review their assets and opportunities for improvement.

Time

10–15 minutes.

What You'll Need

One copy of the handouts on pages 13 through 15 for each participant.

What to Do

Distribute the handouts on pages 13 and 14. Give participants five to ten minutes to complete the activity.

Then distribute the handout on page 15 and ask each participant to develop an action plan to improve two skills.

Tip! You may want to post these action plans in your department and review them on a weekly basis. Reward employees when they make verifiable progress.

If You Have More Time

Make another copy of the Action Plan Worksheet on page 15. Put participants into pairs. Each participant will write the skills he or she wants to improve on the Action Plan Worksheet on the line titled "Your skill." The participants will then trade worksheets with their partners.

Each participant will create an action plan to help his or her partner become a Super Star in the areas listed on the worksheet. Allow five minutes for this activity.

After five minutes, have participants trade action plans and give them several minutes to review.

Discussion Questions

Q: Is it helpful to have someone else brainstorm ideas for you?

A: *Field answers.*

Q: Did your partner think of some ideas that you would not have thought of?

A: *Field answers.*

Ask participants to review their action plans from time to time in order to improve their proficiency in each skill.

Assets and Opportunities

Whether you plan a life-long career in customer service or view your present job as a stepping stone to something else, the skills inherent in providing good customer service will be assets in any field you choose. What's more, a good attitude is key to success anywhere, anytime. Customer service representatives who stand out in their work are:

- Friendly
- Quick
- Efficient
- Eager to please
- Knowledgeable
- Optimistic
- Diligent
- Able to understand customers' requests

- Attentive
- Creatively helpful
- Empathetic
- Poised
- Upbeat
- Honest and fair
- Solution-oriented

These customer service representatives always:

- Listen attentively.
- Maintain a positive attitude.
- Speak clearly.
- Avoid technical terms or fancy words.
- Give customers a feeling of confidence in them, the information they give, and the company.
- Make every customer feel important.
- Soothe ruffled feathers.

Assets and Opportunities

Although you may naturally be stronger in some of the areas than in others, your job provides you the opportunity to master each and every one of these attributes.

Read through the list of assets again and put each item onto the chart below according to your own proficiency. Be honest. No one is watching.

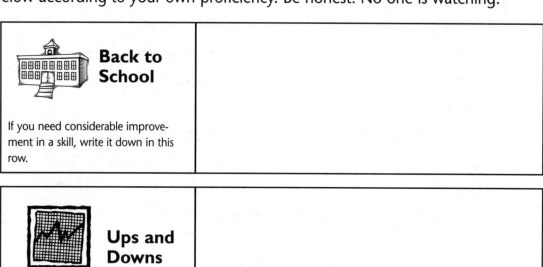

Back to School

If you need considerable improvement in a skill, write it down in this row.

Ups and Downs

If you have average proficiency in a skill, write it here.

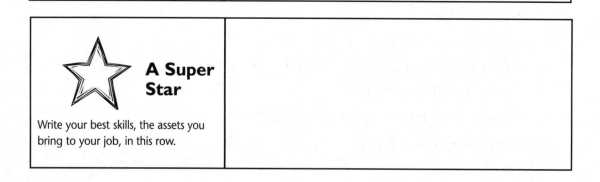

A Super Star

Write your best skills, the assets you bring to your job, in this row.

Action Plan Worksheet

Your skill: _____

Your action plan: _____

_____

_____

_____

_____

_____

_____

_____

Your skill: _____

Your action plan: _____

_____

_____

_____

_____

_____

_____

Write Yourself a Letter

In a Nutshell

Participants write themselves a letter from a fictional customer. Each letter highlights three aspects of the employee's behavior or attitude that made a positive impression on the customer. The letter also points out what effect each action had on the customer. This activity is meant to focus participants' attention on the things they do well, and to motivate them to continue with their efforts.

Time

10–15 minutes.

What You'll Need

One copy of the handouts on pages 19 and 20 for each participant.

What to Do

Distribute the handouts. Read out the sample letter on page 19, and tell participants they'll be writing a similar letter to themselves. Ask them to pay close attention to what the customer says about the impact of the employee's actions and attitude.

Tell participants to think about their own customer service interactions, and how their attitude and behavior affects customers in a positive way. They should complete the form letter on page 20 as if they were a customer. If necessary, they can change the printed words slightly. Give participants about 15 minutes to complete their letters.

Ask for volunteers to read their letters out loud.

Wrap up by pointing out that there are countless ways to serve customers, and even different ways of accomplishing a single objective. Although very few customers actually take the time to write a letter of praise, the participants are serving the needs of customers (and even going beyond at times) during every interaction.

Tip! Copy the sample letter onto an overhead transparency and display it during the letter-writing activity.

Dear Terry:

I wanted to write to thank you personally for the service you provided when I called Atlantis for help with my video camera.

You helped me out in a number of ways. First, you told me about the time delay switch that would allow me to set the camera and then jump into the picture before it started filming. This made me aware of something I didn't even know about my own camera.

I also appreciated the way you took the time to talk me through the whole procedure. Your patience made me feel like a valued customer.

Finally, I wanted to say thanks for telling me about the compact tripod Atlantis offers for this video camera. I think it will really make a difference to my home videos.

Keep up the good work!

Sincerely,

Syd

Syd Matographer

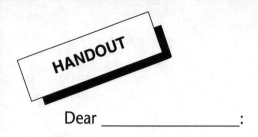

Dear _____:

I wanted to write to thank you personally for the service you provided _____

_____
(when)

_____

You helped me out in a number of ways. First, you _____
(action)
_____ This _____
(effect)

_____

_____

I also appreciated the way you _____
(action)

_____

Your _____
(customer service strength or skill)

made me feel like a valued customer.

Finally, I wanted to say thanks for_____
(action)

I think it will really make a difference to _____
(effect)

Keep up the good work!

Sincerely,

_____
(customer's name)

20

The Best of Times and the Worst of Times

In a Nutshell

In this activity, participants recall and share their real-life experiences—both good and bad—as customers. By highlighting the actions of other customer service providers and the effect of those actions on the participants, the group becomes more aware of what they should and should not do in customer service situations. This is a fun, lively game that works well as a warm-up to a staff meeting or a customer service training session.

Time

15–20 minutes.

What You'll Need

Blank flip-chart paper or white board and markers.

What to Do

Give participants a few moments to think of the best experience they've had when dealing with a customer service representative. Solicit stories from a few people. Be sure they focus on what, specifically, the service person did that led to a good customer service experience. Capture key words on a flip-chart entitled "What to Do."

Next, give participants a few moments to think of the worst experience they've had when dealing with a customer service representative. Solicit stories from a few people. Be sure they focus on what, specifically, the service person did that was wrong. Capture key words on a flip-chart or white board under the heading, "What Not to Do."

2

What You Say and How You Say It

Verbal and Vocal Skills for Customer Service Success

Jargon City

In a Nutshell

Participants focus on identifying words and terms that qualify as jargon or slang. This fast-paced team game helps service employees at all levels of experience become more aware of both common and unusual jargon terms.

Time

15–20 minutes.

What You'll Need

A transparency of the information on page 28, or the definitions copied onto a flip-chart or white board. Participants will need paper and pens.

What to Do

Go over the definitions of jargon and slang to make sure everyone knows what they are.

Divide the participants into teams of two or three. Tell each team to designate one member as the player and another as the recorder. If you divide the group into teams of three, the third member can be a coach to the player, or two players can take turns.

Tell participants that you'll read out several statements from customer service providers in a variety of fields. They should listen carefully to each statement and then follow these directions:

- If the team hears a jargon term they don't understand, the player should stand up and put one hand on his or her head.

- If the team hears a jargon term that they do understand (it's still jargon), the player should put one hand on his or her stomach.

- If the team hears slang, the player should stand on one leg.

Warn participants that each statement may require them to take one, two, or even all three of the positions.

Read the statements out loud, one at a time. Read each statement two times at a normal pace. Give teams a few moments to confer and to take their positions (the recorder should write down the slang and jargon terms) and then call on one team to identify the slang and jargon terms and to say why they took the positions they did. The game should be lively and lighthearted.

Tip! You can enhance this game by including some jargon specific to your company or industry. If possible, take some time before playing the game to write some typical jargon-laden statements that participants might use in conversations with customers. Add these statements to those on page 27.

Jargon City Statements

Jargon and slang terms are underlined.

1. How many <u>meg</u> do you have on your hard drive?

2. What's the <u>OPR code</u> on your mailer?

3. Your system comes with some <u>snap extras</u>: track ball, surge suppressor, glare filter.

4. Just fill out this form, mark your <u>DOB</u>, and give us your <u>ATF</u> and your <u>remit</u>. It's <u>no sweat.</u>

5. With this type of coverage, you're responsible for all <u>copayments</u> and your <u>PAD</u>, <u>CYD</u>, and <u>PDD</u> deductibles.

6. Once you've completed all the documentation, we'll calculate your <u>points</u>. Then we'll figure in your <u>down</u>, and find out if you're eligible for the loan.

7. <u>Gotcha</u>! You'll need a <u>1040EZ</u> and all your <u>W-2s</u>. Don't worry about the self-employment tax; it doesn't apply to you.

jargon (jahr' gun) n. vocabulary specific to a particular trade or profession

examples: chem 7   (a medical test)

              drop ship   (a method of delivering products to buyers)

              four top   (a restaurant table for four people)

slang (slang) n. informal usage in vocabulary that is characteristically more metaphorical, vivid, and playful than ordinary language

examples: buttery   (nice)

              flame   (use e-mail to write disparagingly about someone)

              Yo!   (a greeting)

Stop, Quirk!

In a Nutshell

In this activity, participants listen to audio recordings of themselves in order to identify language quirks that they unconsciously interject into their speech. This activity is ideal for helping employees eliminate annoying speech patterns.

Time

20 minutes.

What You'll Need

Several tape recorders and an audio tape for each two participants (if possible, use tape recorders with handheld microphones). One copy of the handout on page 31 for each participant. Each pair of participants will need a watch (or a clock within plain sight) and a pen.

What to Do

This activity works best if the recording takes place before the participants are aware of what the objective is. Without making reference to what they will be doing later in the session, divide the participants into pairs and ask each pair to complete the following task:

Choose one of the following topics and record yourselves (one at a time) talking freely about the subject for one minute.

- Describe the last movie you saw.
- Describe your most recent vacation or holiday.
- Talk about your personal and professional goals over the next five years.

While one partner speaks, the other should listen, work the tape recorder, and keep track of time. Both partners should make a recording.

Once the pairs have completed their recordings, distribute the handouts, and go over the definition of a quirk to make sure everyone knows what it is. Then ask the pairs to listen to their recordings and identify any quirks that they hear. Quirks aren't limited to the ones identified on the handout.

Next, have the pairs record themselves again, this time choosing another of the three topics and consciously trying to eliminate quirks from their speech.

Ask participants to comment on their progress. Offer them candy or another small reward for their improvement.

quirk (kwurk) n. a peculiarity; a flourish or showy expression; a word or term that annoys and distracts the listener

A quirk is a characteristic of language that draws attention to itself to such an extent that listeners cannot help but be distracted by the annoying quirk. When listeners tune in to quirks, they tend to tune out the true meaning of the communication.

Common quirks include:

Grammar That Makes You Grimace

- Double negatives

  I didn't do nothing.

  That's not right nohow.

- Subject-verb disagreement

  They was in this drawer.

  It don't work that way here.

- Double pronouns

  My boss, he says...

  The production department, they didn't....

Sounds That Make You Squirm

- Sucking sounds
- Lip smacking

Right Word, Weird Usage

Like, I'll see if we can do that.

See, what you have to do is . . .

Expressions From Another Planet

Insofar as

Ain't

Hisself

As it were

What are some quirks you tend to use?

_____

_____

_____

Vocal Charades

In a Nutshell

In this game, participants verbalize written statements using five vocal qualities to enhance the meaning of the text. The objective is for participants to learn how to use their voices to add meaning. This game is especially helpful for employees who deal with customers over the telephone.

Time

10–15 minutes.

What You'll Need

Overhead transparencies or flip-charts of the information on pages 35 and 36.

What to Do

Review the information on page 35 (the numbers refer to what percentage of a message is conveyed by each medium). Remind participants that the customer's impression of them and their organization is influenced significantly by what they say and, even more so, by how they say it (especially on the phone).

Review the overhead on page 36. Remind participants that customers like to hear voices which sound professional, friendly, and confident.

Divide the class into five small groups and quietly assign each group one of the five vocal qualities. Tell the groups not to tell others which vocal skill they have been assigned.

Give the groups a few minutes to decide how to act out or demonstrate their vocal quality. Encourage them to be creative and to make it fun.

After a few minutes, ask each group to demonstrate their vocal quality while the other groups guess which one they were assigned.

Say What?

Face-to-Face Communication

- 55% body language

- 38% tone of voice

- 7% words used

Telephone Communication

- 82% tone of voice

- 18% words used

Albert Mehrabian, Ph.D., UCLA study

Vocal Qualities

Tone

Expresses feeling or emotion

Inflection

Emphasizing words and syllables to enhance message

Pitch

How high or deep voice sounds

Rate

How many words spoken per minute

Volume

How loud or soft voice sounds

In the Studio

In a Nutshell

Participants record themselves and assess the tone, inflection, pitch, rate, and volume of their speech. The objective is for participants to identify areas for improvement. This activity is particularly useful for new and experienced employees who need to improve their vocal skills and for all employees who communicate with customers by telephone.

Time

5 minutes as a group, 5–10 minutes for recording and completing the self-assessment.

What You'll Need

Audio tape recorder(s), blank audio tapes (one per participant), and a timer. One copy of each of the self-assessment handouts on pages 39 and 40 for each participant. If you have not done Vocal Charades, you will also need overhead transparencies or flip-charts of the information on pages 35 and 36.

What to Do

Review the information on the overhead on page 35 and remind participants that the customer's impression of them and their organization is influenced by what they say and, even more so, by how they say it.

Review the five vocal qualities on the overhead on page 36. Remind participants that customers like to hear voices which sound professional, friendly, and confident.

Arrange for participants to have access to a tape recorder and audio tape. Hand out copies of the assessments on pages 39 and 40.

If You Have More Time

Reconvene participants. Debrief the exercise. Ask them what they learned and have them complete the Personal Action Plan on page 15 for two vocal skills they would like to improve.

Recording I

Instructions:

Choose a long passage from your company brochure or other related material and record yourself reading for one minute. Read as if you were talking to a customer; that is, try to keep the rate of your speech even and moderate. At the end of one minute, stop reading and count the number of words you read. Try this exercise three times with three different passages and record the number of words you read.

Words per minute:

_____

_____

_____

If you're in the range of 160 to 180 words per minute, you speak at a rate that is comfortable for your customers. If your rate is consistently above or below this range, make a point of working on your rate of speech.

Recording 2

Instructions:

Choose several other long passages from your company brochure or other related material. Record yourself reading the passage out loud as if you were talking to a customer.

Listen to the recording and pay close attention to the tone, inflection, pitch, rate, and volume of your voice. For each of the characteristics listed below, place an "x" on the line in the location that corresponds to what you hear on the tape (see the first line as an example).

Happy	✗	*Sad*
Non-nasal		*Nasal*
Slow		*Fast*
Soft		*Loud*
Neutral		*Whiny*
Neutral		*Sarcastic*
Deep		*Shrill*
Monotonous		*Dramatic*

Take notes on aspects you want to improve and re-record until you are satisfied. If you'd like, you can ask one or two co-workers to listen to the tape and give you their opinion.

Let Me Tell You What I **Can** Do

In a Nutshell

This activity teaches customer service employees what to say and do when they have to turn down a customer's request or deliver other bad news. It's suitable for employees of all levels.

Time

15–20 minutes.

What You'll Need

One copy of the handouts on pages 43 and 44 for each participant.

What to Do

Distribute the handouts and review the one on page 43 with the group. Let participants work in groups of two or three to complete the exercise on page 44.

Ask participants to share their answers. Make sure the answers follow the three steps listed on the handout on page 43. Ask participants to post the handout near their desks to refer to until they have mastered this skill.

Answers

Here are some possible answers:

1. It's against federal regulations for me to release that information to you. However, we do have a waiver that your ex-wife can sign that would allow us to release her account information to the people she lists on the waiver. Would you like me to give you one of those to have her to fill out?

2. I'm unable to send the flowers without pre-payment, but you don't have to come into the store to pay if that's not convenient for you. We take MasterCard®, Visa®, and American Express®. Or, if you'd like to drop a check in the mail, we'll send the flowers out just as soon as it arrives.

3. Before you start the weight loss program, we'd like you to make an appointment to be evaluated by one of our dieticians. We've found that people who meet with the dietician first maintain their weight loss over a longer period of time. We have appointments in the evenings and on Saturday if that would be more convenient for you than during the week.

If You Have More Time

Ask participants to brainstorm situations in which they have to say "no" to their customers. Have participants work in small groups and use the three steps to craft responses. Ask participants to share their responses with the rest of the group.

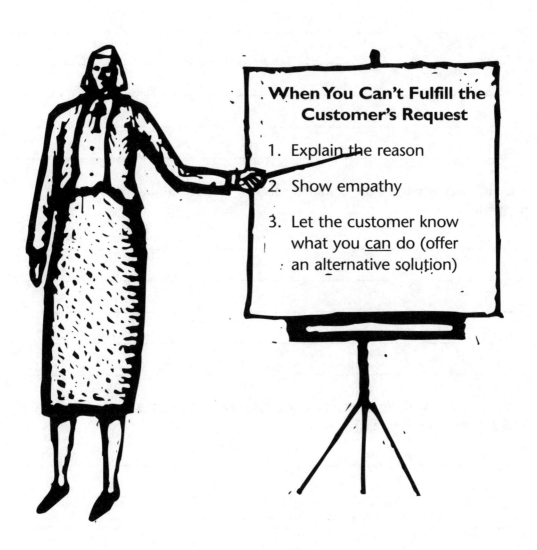

When You Can't Fulfill the Customer's Request

1. Explain the reason

2. Show empathy

3. Let the customer know what you <u>can</u> do (offer an alternative solution)

43

What would you say to the customer if you found yourself in the following situations? Use the three-step model to communicate this information to the customer.

1. You can't give the customer information on his ex-wife's account balance because it would be illegal.

_____

_____

_____

_____

_____

2. You can't wire flowers to the customer's sister in Boston without first receiving payment.

_____

_____

_____

_____

_____

3. You can't sell weight loss products to the customer because she must first be evaluated by your dieticians.

_____

_____

_____

_____

_____

3

Make the Connection

Training Games for Telephone Success

Getting Around

In a Nutshell

During this activity, participants learn what to say when they put a caller on hold or transfer a call. This activity is suitable for establishing a company-wide policy, for training new hires, and as a refresher course.

Time

10–15 minutes.

What You'll Need

One copy of the handout on page 48 for each participant.

What to Do

Distribute one handout to each participant and review the handout. Ask participants for situations in which they need to transfer the call or put a caller on hold.

Put participants in groups of two: one participant is the caller, the other participant is the customer service representative. Ask them to choose from the situations just developed to practice these two skills, and to alternate roles.

Have participants post the handout in their work areas until they master these skills.

Putting a Caller On Hold
1. Explain why
2. Ask permission
3. Put caller on hold
4. Thank the caller for holding

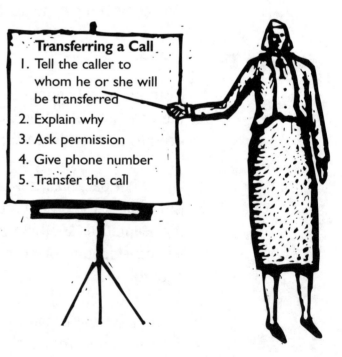

Transferring a Call
1. Tell the caller to whom he or she will be transferred
2. Explain why
3. Ask permission
4. Give phone number
5. Transfer the call

Outbound Excellence

In a Nutshell

Participants review two scenarios to identify elements of both good and bad communication in the outbound telephone service environment. The objective is for participants to learn to avoid the common errors and annoyances associated with outbound calls. This game is suitable for anyone who calls customers.

Time

20–30 minutes.

What You'll Need

One copy of the handouts on pages 51 through 53 for each participant. One copy of the handout on page 35 for each participant if you have not already done Vocal Charades in Chapter 2. A blank flip-chart or white board and marker pens.

What to Do

Discuss telephone communication with participants. Remind them of the information on the handout on page 35 and of the importance of telephone communication in building a long-lasting relationship with customers.

Advise participants that there are other factors to keep in mind when contacting customers by phone. Distribute the handout on page 51. Have participants work in groups of three or four to complete the exercise.

After about five minutes, reconvene the group and ask participants what helps and hindrances they noticed. List them on a flip-chart or white board.

Distribute the handout on page 52. Have participants work in groups of three or four to complete the exercise.

After about five minutes, reconvene the group and ask participants what helps and hindrances they noticed. List them on a flip-chart or white board.

You should now have a master list of desirable behaviors for successful outbound telephone calls. This list should contain the information on the handout on page 53 as well as any other items offered by the participants.

Distribute the handout on page 53. Ask participants to post it near their desks until they have mastered the skills listed.

Instructions:

Read the following scenario and note what the customer service representative does to facilitate good communication and what she does to hinder it.

Emily Ng, a customer service representative with Midtown Telephone Company has a note on her desk from a co-worker that says: "John Dawson called at 11:30. He said you were supposed to call him at 10:00 to explain the charges on his first bill." Here's the transcript of Emily's call:

Emily: Hi. This is Emily. Did you have a question?

John: Emily? *(John sounds lost.)*

Emily: Yeah, Emily from the phone company. Was I supposed to call you earlier?

John: Yes, you were. You were supposed to do some research and explain these charges on my bill. They aren't what I agreed to when I signed up for your service.

Emily: *(Emily sighs loudly.)* Well, I've really been busy and I didn't have time to figure it out. I'm sorry. What's your account number?

John: Emily, I'm in a meeting now. Can you call me back this afternoon?

Emily: Sure. Talk to you later. *(Emily hangs up; John stares at the receiver in disbelief.)*

Instructions:

Read the following scenario and note what the customer service representative does to facilitate good communication and what she does to hinder it.

Maggie Sanchez from Xeno, Inc. called Over-the-Wire Telephone Company to find out why Xeno's bill was so much higher than usual that month. Her account representative, Elliot, said he would research the problem and call Maggie back at 9:00 the following morning. Here's a transcript of the call:

Elliot: Good morning, Maggie. This is Elliot Liebmann at Over-the-Wire. I have some information for you about your phone bill and I wonder if this is a good time to go over it with you.

Maggie: Morning, Elliot. You're right on time; I was waiting for your call. What have you found out?

Elliot: Well, I have a copy of your bill right here. Do you have your bill handy?

Maggie: Yes, it's right here. Did you find out why it was so high this month?

Elliot: Yes, I did. Turn to page four and look at the last line on the page. We made a mistake and added some access charges that we shouldn't have. I really apologize for our mistake. To correct it, we'll issue you a credit for $468.23 so all you have to pay this month is $823.46. Will that rectify the problem?

Maggie: Yes it will. Thanks so much for your help with this, Elliot.

Elliot: No problem. That credit should show up on your bill next month. And if you have any other questions, please give me a call. My direct number is 555-8663.

Tips for Successful Outbound Calls

- Identify yourself, your company, and the reason for your call.

- Call when you say you will.

- Have all the information you need at hand before you place the call.

- Ask if it's a good time for the customer to speak with you.

- Tell the customer what to expect next (if appropriate).

Oops Theater

In a Nutshell

Participants take turns playing out telephone customer service situations while others play the
role of critic. The objective is for participants to recognize
the hallmarks of superior telephone customer service.
This game is suitable for employees who need to practice
telephone communication skills.

Time

5–10 minutes.

What You'll Need

Two copies each of the handouts on pages 57 and 58.
A blank flip-chart or white board and markers.

What to Do

Ask for four volunteers to be "actors." Put actors in pairs,
and give each pair two copies of the script (one pair gets
Scenario #1 and the other gets Scenario #2). Give the
actors a minute or two to determine who will play which
part and to review their roles.

Ask the "audience" to pay close attention to what each
customer service representative does and how it affects
the customer. Ask the first pair to act out Scenario #1, and

then ask for the audience's comments. Then do the same for Scenario #2. Ask participants to suggest improvements. Following are some possibilities:

Scenario #1:
- Answer phone sooner.
- Give a proper greeting with offer of assistance.
- Offer to be of assistance, not just send information.
- Say "please" when requesting information.
- Be prepared to receive a call by having a paper and pencil handy.
- Be more polite and professional.
- Confirm the caller's address.
- Use a proper closing.

Scenario #2:
- Don't be defensive.
- Don't blame the caller.
- Empathize with the caller's situation.

If You Have More Time

Ask for four new volunteers to act out revised versions of the scenarios. Give the new actors copies of the scenarios and allow them a few minutes to prepare, then have them give their performance. Ask the audience for comments.

Scenario #1

Instructions: Read through the script below. Decide who will play the part of the employee and who will play the part of the caller. Review your role to prepare for your "performance."

Caller: *(Make the sound of a phone ringing four times.)*

Employee: *(Sounding rushed and preoccupied)*
Super-Tech, Alex here.

Caller: Yes, hello. I'm calling to get some information on your computer classes.

Employee: *(Sounding in a hurry)*
Yeah, OK. What's your address? Oh, wait a minute, I can't find anything to write on. OK. I'm with ya now. OK. Go.

Caller: It's 463 Spring Street. The zip over here is 93355.

Employee: OK. Got it. Thanks.
(Hang up)

Scenario #2

Instructions: Read through the script below. Decide who will play the part of the employee and who will play the part of the caller. Review your role to prepare for your "performance."

Caller: *(Make the sound of a phone ringing.)*

Employee: *(Sounding pleasant and glad the caller called)*
            Paper Warehouse. This is <your name>. How can I help you today?

Caller: Hi. This is Terry with Town Square Printing, and I ordered 27 reams of paper for a printing project that's due in two days and it hasn't arrived!

Employee: *(Sounding unsure of what to do)*
            Yeah?

Caller: I have to get this project started right away or it won't be finished in time, and I just can't go out and buy the paper retail because it's a special stock that only your company has available.

Employee: *(Sounding defensive)*
            Oh, well, I don't know what happened. I mean, I didn't handle that order. Are you sure you told us when you needed it?

Caller: *(Sounding angry)*
            Forget it. I'll get it somewhere else.
            (Hang up)

Tennis Shoe Alien

In a Nutshell

This is a fun, lively game in which participants verbally instruct an "alien" to put on a sock and tennis shoe—they aren't able to demonstrate. The objective is for participants to learn to give clear instructions. This game is ideally suited to employees who need to give instructions to customers over the telephone.

Time

15–20 minutes.

What You'll Need

A pair of socks and a pair of tennis shoes (in your size); one tennis shoe should be unlaced. One copy of the handout on page 61 for each participant.

What to Do

You will play the part of the alien. Enter the room with one sock and laced shoe on one foot; the other foot is bare. Distribute the handouts to the participants. Sit down and drop the sock, lace, and shoe in front of you and wait for instructions.

Your job is to help participants realize that they must give explicit instructions. Do not speak and do

<u>exactly</u> what you are instructed to do. If a participant says "Put the sock on your foot," pick up the sock and lay it on top of your foot. If the participant says "Pick up the lace," pick it up in the middle, not at the end. If the participant says "Put the lace in the hole of the shoe," put just the tip of the lace in any hole, not necessarily the first one—or put the lace inside the shoe.

If several participants shout instructions at once, or if a participant becomes overly emotional or frustrated or calls you names, you can shut down. Just slump over! You can come back to life again if participants say or do something that makes you want to continue to participate.

After ten minutes, stop the activity and ask the discussion questions. If time permits, continue with the activity. Participants should be much better at giving instructions the second time around.

Discussion Questions

Q: What did you learn about giving instructions?

A: *Field answers.*

Q: In this case you could see that the alien was or was not following your instructions. How do you know if the customer is following instructions when you're on the phone?

A: *Ask confirming questions.*

Q: How can you give better instructions to your customers?

A: *Field answers.*

Tennis Shoe Alien

The "person" who has just handed you this is an alien from another planet. Before arriving, the alien was properly shod with shoes and socks on both feet. However, being curious about our ways, the alien has pulled off one shoe and sock and doesn't know how to put it back on.

Being the kindhearted earthling that you are, you want to help the alien lace the shoe and put the sock and laced shoe back on. Your job is to give explicit instructions for the alien to follow. (The alien received a crash course in English as a second language before arriving, but doesn't speak at all.)

The alien is not able to copy you, so demonstrating with your own shoe and sock will not be of any help. Also, the alien has evolved in such a way that it can only hear one person speak at a time. Please work with the other participants in your class so that you take turns giving instructions.

Oh yes, a few words of warning . . . do not touch the alien. If you do, well, there are no guarantees. The last person who touched the alien was immediately vaporized.

Are You Alive?

In a Nutshell

In this game, participants practice using transitions to avoid long, awkward periods of silence when talking to customers on the phone or in person. This game is ideal for anyone who has frequent or long pauses during transactions with customers.

Time

10–15 minutes.

What You'll Need

One copy of handout on page 65 for each pair of participants. A small, light ball (a small pillow or stuffed animal will work).

What to Do

Divide participants into pairs and give each pair a copy of the handout. Tell them the purpose of this activity is to practice using transitions to avoid "dead air" when talking to customers either on the phone or in person. Allow them five minutes to complete the handout.

After five minutes, have all the participants stand in a circle a few feet from one another. Tell them to toss the ball around; whoever catches the ball has to use a transition statement and then toss the ball to someone else.

Discussion Questions

Q. Why is it important to communicate with customers rather than allow long periods of silence?

A: *Customers don't always know what you're doing. By communicating with them as you process their requests, you reassure them that you haven't forgotten about them, and you keep them informed about the process. Customers love to be "in the loop."*

Q. When do you need to use transitions in your own customer service interactions?

A: *Answers will vary.*

Q. If you're talking to a customer on the phone, when should you put them on hold and when should you use transitions while keeping the customer on the line?

A. *Standard practice is to put a customer on hold if you're going to take more than one minute to find the information or process the request. Remember to always ask the customer's permission before using the hold button!*

Transitions

"One moment please."

There's nothing wrong with this phrase, but it sure doesn't communicate much to the customer—only that he or she needs to wait. We know you can do better than that.

What are some alternative statements you can use to communicate with customers when you're handling their requests?

Example: *Mrs. Jones, it will take me a minute or two to find that information in my files.*

1. _____

   _____

2. _____

   _____

3. _____

   _____

4. _____

   _____

5. _____

   _____

4

Here's Looking at You

Games for Excellence in the Face-to-Face Service Environment

Let Me Count the Ways

In a Nutshell

Participants work in groups to come up with as many differences between phone and face-to-face customer service as they can. They then brainstorm ways to use these differences to their customers' advantage. This game is best for employees who deal with customers predominantly in the face-to-face environment or in both the telephone and face-to-face environments.

Time

15–20 minutes.

What You'll Need

One copy of the handouts on pages 71 and 72 for every three participants. A flip-chart and markers.

What to Do

Divide participants into groups of two or three and give each group one copy of the handout on page 71. Tell them to take five minutes to brainstorm as many differences as they can between the telephone and face-to-face customer service environments. They should focus on completing the following sentence:

In the face-to-face customer service environment, . . .

The most obvious difference, of course, is that in the face-to-face environment, the customer can see you. Participants should break this down into more subtle distinctions—for example, the customer can see what you're wearing.

At this point, the participants should focus only on coming up with conditions of the face-to-face environment (part one of the handout). Later, they'll have an opportunity to discuss how these conditions influence their customer service (part two of the handout).

After five minutes, stop the brainstorming session and ask each group to report one of their findings. Continue until each group has reported all the differences on their list. Capture these findings on a flip-chart as you go.

Then divide the findings, assign each group one share, and distribute the handout on page 72. Their new assignment is to turn each condition into a "rule." For example: Because customers can see what you're wearing, you should always dress appropriately and professionally.

After three or four minutes, ask each group to report their "rules."

Part One

In the face-to-face customer service environment, . . .

1. customers can see what you're wearing

2.

3.

4.

5.

6.

7.

8.

9.

10.

Part 2

1. Because *customers can see what you're wearing*
   (condition of face-to-face service)
   you should dress appropriately
   (what you should do to give good service)

2. Because _____

   _____.

3. Because _____

   _____.

4. Because _____

   _____.

5. Because _____

   _____.

6. Because _____

First Impressions

In a Nutshell

This is a consciousness-raising game for customer service providers at all levels. Participants examine their own biases and impressions based on people's appearances, and then discuss what impressions customers might have of *them*, based on their appearance.

Time

10–15 minutes.

What You'll Need

Select several (at least five per group) photographs of people from magazines or print advertisements. The photographs should represent as diverse a population as possible. The photos should not portray famous or recognizable people.

What to Do

Divide participants into groups of three or four and give each group several photographs to examine. Tell them to discuss among themselves what impressions they have of these people based solely on how they look in the photograph.

After about five minutes, ask for some volunteers to briefly report each group's impressions. Then tell them to think about and discuss what impressions customers might have of them (the participants) based on how they look.

Emphasize to participants that the objective of this game is not to debate whether or not these first impressions are fair. Participants should focus solely on what impression their appearance makes on customers.

Tip! Keep the magazine pictures in a file for future use. You can add to the file whenever you come across appropriate photographs in magazines.

You might like to mention to participants that it's been suggested by experts that employees should always dress as if they held a job one level above their current status. This makes a favorable impression on customers and on managers, and may help them win consideration for promotions.

You Look Marvelous!

In a Nutshell

In this game, participants review various pictures to determine the importance of body language and appearance in adding meaning to communication. The objective is for participants to learn basic techniques they can use to be sure their body language and appearance are sending the message they intend. This game is ideal for introducing the concept of visual communication.

Time

10–15 minutes.

What You'll Need

One copy of the handout on page 77 for each participant. A blank flip-chart or white board and marker.

What to Do

Distribute one copy of the handout to each participant. Ask participants to work in small groups to determine what they think each person does for a living and what each person is feeling. They should also discuss why they came to these conclusions.

After five to seven minutes, ask each group to report their findings. List any points they made regarding body language and attire on the flip-chart or white board.

Discussion Questions

Q: How do your body language and attire affect your communication with your customer?

A: *A customer can tell you are friendly, confident, and interested if you dress appropriate to your position, if you maintain an open stance, and if you lean back slightly to show you're relaxed or lean forward slightly to indicate you're interested (Figures 4 and 5). A customer may perceive you as defensive if you close up and cross your arms (Figure 1). A customer may show you that he or she is angry or upset by maintaining a frontal, rigid stance (Figures 2 and 3).*

Q: What kind of posture can you exhibit to help defuse a challenging situation, such as when a customer is complaining or making unfair accusations?

A: *Keep an open posture and lean forward slightly to show that you are interested in helping the customer find a solution.*

Q: What, if anything, would you like to change about your body language or attire to help you provide better service to your customers?

A: *Field answers.*

Figure 1

Figure 2

Figure 3

Figure 4

Figure 5

Figure 6

Face Off

In a Nutshell

Some participants demonstrate facial expressions while other participants guess which emotion is being conveyed. The objective is for participants to learn the importance of facial expressions in adding meaning to their communication with customers. This game is suitable for employees who want to improve their recognition of the meaning behind various facial expressions.

Time

10–15 minutes.

What You'll Need

One copy of the handout on page 81. A flip-chart or white board with the following words posted: happy, sad, pleasantly surprised, unpleasantly surprised, anxious, angry, concerned, bored, in a hurry, interested. A stopwatch or watch that displays seconds.

What to Do

Cut along the dotted lines of the handout. Divide participants into two teams, and give each team five slips of paper. Explain that their job is to select an actor or actors to demonstrate each of the emotions through facial expression only.

Give teams a couple of minutes to prepare, then have a "face-off." During the "face-off" teams face each other. The actor on Team One acts out one of the emotions by using facial expressions; the other team gets 15 seconds to confer and decide which emotion Team One is demonstrating. Team Two then demonstrates another emotion, and teams alternate until all emotions have been demonstrated.

If You Have More Time

Have actors replay their demonstrations. After each demonstration, ask the class how they knew which emotion the actor was demonstrating. Have them pay particular attention to the actor's forehead, eyebrows, eyes, mouth, and tilt of head.

Discuss the implications of various facial expressions for participants in their jobs.

HANDOUT

HAPPY	**SAD**
PLEASANTLY SURPRISED	**UNPLEASANTLY SURPRISED**
ANXIOUS	**ANGRY**
CONCERNED	**BORED**
IN A HURRY	**INTERESTED**

Five Pillars of Success

In a Nutshell

This is a role-play game in which participants identify five basic communication skills that are essential to success in face-to-face customer service. It's ideal for employees who need to polish their face-to-face communication skills.

Time

10–15 minutes.

What You'll Need

Two copies of the handouts on pages 85 and 86.

What to Do

Ask for two volunteer "actors" to role play in front of the group. Assign each actor a role and give them both a script. Give them a few moments to look over their roles, and then ask them to play out their customer service encounter (Take One). Tell the rest of the group to pay close attention to what the actors do and how it affects the interaction.

After the interaction, ask what they noticed. Then have the actors role-play Take Two, and ask the rest of the group to look for five things that the customer service representative does that have a positive influence on the customer.

Debrief the role-play by asking the audience to identify five things that the customer service rep did well. They may come up with more than five, but they should identify the following: Greet the customer, make eye contact, smile, use open body language, and thank the customer.

Discussion Questions

Q: Why should you greet the customer?

A: *It's common courtesy, and it shows your willingness to serve.*

Q: Why is it important to make eye contact?

A: *Making eye contact reassures customers that your attention is focused on them.*

Q: Why smile?

A: *You'll put the customer at ease, and you'll be more relaxed and eager to serve. You'll also make the customer feel valued.*

Q: What is the importance of using open body language? What are some examples of open body language?

A: *Open body language tells customers you're willing to help them and it helps establish a rapport. Some examples of open body language are facing the customer, uncrossing your arms, relaxing your posture, and looking at the customer when he or she talks.*

Q: Why thank the customer?

A: *It shows courtesy for the customer and reinforces that you value the customer's business.*

Take One

This brief role-play takes place at a travel agency. In this first scene, the customer service representative (CSR) is friendly and helpful, but neglects to do five important things:

- Smile

- Greet the customer

- Use open body language

- Make eye contact

- Thank the customer

Customer: Hi!

CSR: (Looks up as customer walks in, but doesn't smile or say anything)

Customer: Uhh, I wanted to get some information about Caribbean cruises.

CSR: (Uses a friendly voice but with arms crossed and doesn't look directly at the customer . . .)

Sure. We offer several options. Would you like some brochures, or did you want me to look up availability and pricing information?

Customer: Well, right now I'd just like some brochures to take home and review. We're not planning to go until next year.

CSR: No problem. Here are some brochures for you (Hands them to customer). You can take a look at them and give me a call if you have any questions.

Customer: Great. Thank you.

CSR: Sure.

(Customer turns and walks away)

Take Two

This is a reenactment of the first role-play, but this time the customer service representative (CSR) remembers to do all five of the following:

- Smile
- Greet the customer
- Use open body language
- Make eye contact
- Thank the customer

CSR: *(Looks up as customer walks in, and smiles)*
Good morning.

Customer: Hi!

CSR: *(Facing customer and making eye contact)*
What can I do for you?

Customer: Well, I wanted to get some information about Caribbean cruises.

CSR: OK. We offer several options. Would you like some brochures, or did you want me to look up availability and pricing information?

Customer: Well, right now I'd just like some brochures to take home and review. We're not planning to go until next year.

CSR: No problem. Here are some brochures for you *(Hands them to customer)*. You can take a look at them and give me a call if you have any questions.

Customer: Great! Thank you.

CSR: Thank you for stopping by.

(Customer turns and walks away)

5

Make It a Great Day

Games for Establishing Rapport with Every Customer

Hidden Rapport

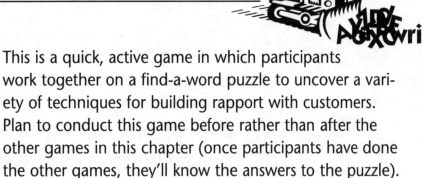

In a Nutshell

This is a quick, active game in which participants work together on a find-a-word puzzle to uncover a variety of techniques for building rapport with customers. Plan to conduct this game before rather than after the other games in this chapter (once participants have done the other games, they'll know the answers to the puzzle). This game is ideal for new hires, but can be used as a refresher for employees at all levels.

Time

10–15 minutes.

What You'll Need

One copy of the handout on page 91 for each pair of participants.

What to Do

Ask someone to define "rapport." Divide the participants into pairs and tell them they'll be working with their partners to uncover several techniques for building rapport with customers.

Hand out the puzzle and give them about ten minutes to complete it. Go over the answers as a group.

Answers

1. Use the customer's NAME.
2. Say PLEASE and THANK YOU when asking customers for INFORMATION.
3. Explain your REASONS when you have to say NO to a customer's request.
4. Show your INTEREST in the customer's needs.
5. Show EMPATHY for the customer's FEELINGS.
6. Let the customer know what his or her OPTIONS are.
7. SMILE! Even if you're on the phone!

Rapport Puzzle

There are countless ways to build rapport with customers. The puzzle below contains words that complete the following rapport-building techniques. We've done the first one for you.

1. Use the customer's <u>N</u> <u>A</u> <u>M</u> <u>E</u>.
2. Say _ _ _ _ _ _ _ and _ _ _ _ _ _ _ _ _ when asking customers for _ _ _ _ _ _ _ _ _ _ _ _.
3. Explain your _ _ _ _ _ _ _ _ when you have to say _ _ to a customer's request.
4. Show your _ _ _ _ _ _ _ _ _ in the customer's needs.
5. Show _ _ _ _ _ _ _ for the customer's _ _ _ _ _ _ _ _.
6. Let the customer know what his or her _ _ _ _ _ _ _ _ are.
7. _ _ _ _ _ _! Even if you're on the phone!

Words can appear horizontally, vertically, or diagonally, and may go in any direction.

```
R   M   I   I   K   S   L   E   R   S   T
O   P   M   K   Y   R   E   J   S   W   E
O   T   R   E   E   L   C   N   H   E   E
T   H   A   N   K   Y   O   U   A   S   M
S   E   R   R   A   S   P   B   G   A   P
E   M   A   N   A   A   T   N   M   E   A
R   D   I   E   L   D   I   A   P   L   T
E   Q   R   L   O   L   O   W   I   P   H
T   I   R   E   E   O   N   N   U   Y   Y
N   O   W   E   R   H   S   A   E   L   P
I   N   F   O   R   M   A   T   I   O   N
```

I Feel for You

In a Nutshell

In this game, participants work in pairs to rewrite dry, rote statements to show more empathy for customers. This game is useful for new hires or as a refresher for seasoned service employees.

Time

15–20 minutes.

What You'll Need

An overhead transparency or flip-chart of the information on page 95. One copy of pages 96 and 97 cut so that you have seven slips of paper, each with one scenario. Put these in a "hat" (a small basket or bowl will do).

What to Do

Read out the following scenario and ask participants which response sounds better and why.

A customer calls and says, "My home was damaged in the earthquake and I need to know what the insurance will cover." Which of the following two responses do you think the customer would prefer to hear?

1. If you give me your policy number, I'll check your coverage.

2. I'm sorry to hear you were affected by the earthquake. If you'll let me know your policy number, I'll check the extent of your coverage.

Ask participants what the second customer service representative did that the first one didn't. (Showed empathy for the customer's situation.) Show the overhead or flip-chart to the group, and briefly go over the definition of empathy.

Tell participants that it isn't necessary for them to express empathy in every customer service interaction, but when a customer is in a difficult situation, it's essential that they show their concern. There are many ways to show empathy for customers—through actions, words, tone of voice, etc.

Divide participants into pairs. Ask each pair to come to the front of the room and draw a statement out of the hat. One partner should read the customer's statement and the other should read the customer service representative's response. Each of the other pairs has to quickly come up with a rewrite of the customer service representative's response to show more empathy for the customer. Have each pair share their response with the group, and then ask the next pair to come draw from the hat. Answers will vary, but you should make sure each rewritten response conveys empathy for the customer.

Tip! If competitions work well with your group, you can offer a small prize to the pair who comes up with the best rewrite of each response.

empathy (em' pe thee) n. identification with or vicarious experiencing of the feelings, thoughts, or attitudes of another person

To show empathy for customers, you might use the following phrases:

I understand...

I'm sorry...

I can appreciate...

Empathy is also conveyed by your tone of voice and body language.

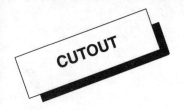

Customer: I have tickets to the evening performance on the 15th, but unfortunately I broke my leg a few days ago and won't be able to go until my cast is off. Is it possible to exchange my tickets for some other show later in the season?

CSR: It depends what kind of tickets you bought. Do you have the tickets handy?

Customer: I brought my car in for an estimate this morning—it got banged up in an accident. I'm calling to see if it's ready. The name's Johnson.

CSR: I'll check; what type of car is it?

Customer: Hi. I came in here yesterday afternoon to take care of some paperwork. I noticed last night that my wallet is missing, so I'm retracing my steps to see if I can find it. I don't know yet if it's been stolen or just misplaced. Did you happen to find a lost wallet?

CSR: Bummer. I'll check our Lost and Found.

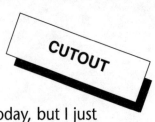

Customer: I have an appointment with the dentist for 3:00 today, but I just found out that I have to make a 2:00 flight to New York. Is there any possibility I can see the dentist sooner? I've had a toothache for two days and I hate to let it go until I get back from New York.

CSR: Well, we try to leave some openings for emergencies. Let me see if the dentist can fit you in sooner.

Customer: My hard disk crashed—I think because of a virus that came in through my Internet connection—and I need to know how to retrieve my data. It's all gone, and I don't have copies of everything.

CSR: There's a good chance we can fix it, but it may take some time. Let me ask you a few questions about your system and then I'll tell you what to do.

Customer: My doctor has put me on a very strict diet and I don't see anything on the menu that I can eat. Is it possible to get some steamed vegetables and rice?

CSR: Well, I'll have to check with the chef. I don't know if we can do special orders.

Customer: I just realized that I gave you the wrong materials to print! If I run back to the office and get the right ones, can you still do the order by noon?

CSR: Oh man! We'll see what we can do; how soon can you get back here?

Accentuate the Positive

In a Nutshell

In this game, participants practice "showing value"—that is, letting customers know how they will benefit from the way their requests and needs are handled. This game is suitable for anyone in customer service, and works best with a group of 10–16 participants.

Time

10–15 minutes.

What You'll Need

One copy of page 102, cut along the dotted lines to create game cards. Keep the two types of cards separate; "procedures" in roman text go to Team A and "values" in italic text go to Team B. You'll also need a flip-chart or white board and marker pens.

What to Do

Write the following on a flip-chart or white board and keep it covered until you're ready to explain the concept to participants:

To Show Value...
Always look for the positive aspects of customer service situations and point these out to customers.

Read out the following two statements and ask participants why the second one sounds so much better.

1. You'll have to come in to one of our service facilities to have the work done.

2. To keep your costs down, we ask that you have the work done at one of our service facilities.

Let's try another one:

1. We can't give out identification numbers over the phone; it's against our policy.

2. To protect the privacy of our customers, we don't give out identification numbers over the telephone.

Explain to participants that in the second statement of each situation, the customer service representative did more than just tell the customer why. The second statement shows the value of the policy or procedure. This is an important step in building rapport with customers. The value isn't always obvious, but almost every policy and procedure is of some value to customers. If you look for it, you can find it. Showing value can also smooth ruffled feathers. Notice the difference between these two statements:

1. You'll have to vacate your home for two days while the termite control procedure is in progress.

2. Most pest control companies spray only once, but we spray three times. You'll need to be out of your home for two days while we do this, but spraying three times guarantees we'll get all the termites.

Tell participants that now it's their turn to practice showing value. Divide the group into two teams, A and B.

Distribute the "procedures" (roman text) to Team A and the "values" (italic text) to Team B. Each participant should get only one card. (Note: There are enough cards for sixteen players. If you have fewer than sixteen, eliminate some of the procedure cards and their corresponding value cards.)

Tell participants to circulate around the room and try to identify their partner by matching a procedure to a corresponding value. Once they've met their match, they should work together to come up with a statement that shows value to the customer.

Reconvene the group and ask pairs to read their statements out loud.

If You Have More Time

Hold a discussion about the value of your organization's procedures and ask participants to write some statements for showing value to their own customers. We suggest you create a list of your organization's procedures ahead of time and then ask participants to come up with corresponding value statements.

CUTOUT

Procedures:	Values:
You don't ship by regular mail; you use only expedited shipping.	*This ensures that your food products are delivered fresh.*
You have to collect the zip code of every customer.	*This helps you to know where to plan new stores in the future that will be convenient for customers.*
You ask for a credit card number so that the monthly charge can be billed to the customer's card.	*This ensures that there won't be any delay in getting your monthly supply of merchandise to you.*
Your search takes at least five days.	*Yours is one of the most exhaustive book search services in the country, with over 4000 sources.*
You don't give out estimates over the phone.	*This helps you to give customers a fair and accurate quote.*
You don't send out diet products until the customer has been evaluated by your in-house physicians.	*This ensures safe and healthy use of the products.*
You don't keep stock in the store; it's kept in a warehouse until delivery.	*This keeps overhead costs down and allows you to pass on the savings to your customers.*
You're required to put a two-day hold on computerized checks.	*This cuts down on fraud.*

And How's the Weather?

In a Nutshell

Participants learn to pick up clues from customers that can help them to build a strong rapport. This game is designed for employees in the face-to-face customer service environment and is especially helpful for those who have difficulty making light, easy conversation with customers.

Note: This game should be played by participants who are familiar with the concept of rapport.

Time

10–15 minutes.

What You'll Need

Prepare for this game by cutting out of magazines photographs of people in everyday life situations (you'll need 7-10 photos for each group of participants). The people in the photographs should not be famous or recognizable. By combing a variety of publications, you should be able to find a diverse representation of fictional customers.

Tip! After the game, collect the photographs and keep them on file for future use. You can add to the collection as you come across interesting photographs in magazines.

What to Do

Briefly discuss the concept of rapport. Tell participants that in this game they will practice picking up clues from customers that can help them build a strong rapport.

Divide the participants into groups of two or three. Give each group a selection of "customer" photographs and ask them to study the photos and come up with statements they might use to make pleasant, light conversation with customers. Each statement should have some relevance to the photograph. Give them an example by holding up a photo and suggesting two or three statements you might make to the customer.

Let's say for example, you had a photo of a man in a Denver Broncos shirt with three children in tow. You might say:

- *How old are your children?*
- *Are you a Broncos fan?*
- *Sounds like you all had quite a winter in Denver this year!*

After about ten minutes, ask the groups to share one or two of their photos and accompanying statements with the rest of the participants.

Now That's Rapport!

In a Nutshell

Participants read a case study of a customer service interaction in which the employee did a great job. They have to identify what the customer service representative did to build a strong rapport with the customer. This game is suitable for all employees who need to learn to develop rapport with customers.

Time

10–15 minutes.

What You'll Need

One copy of the handouts on pages 107 and 108 for each participant.

What to Do

Give one copy of the handout on page 107 to each participant and ask them to read it.

Review the handout on page 108 with participants. Ask participants to work in groups of two or three to review the scenario on page 107 and underline the passages that show what the customer service representative said to build a good rapport with the customer.

Review each group's answers and discuss as needed.

Ask participants to keep a copy of page 108 in their workstations until they've mastered the skill of building rapport.

FRIENDLY FRAN: Thank you for calling Global Village Airlines. This is Fran. How may I help you?

TRAVELIN' TRAVIS: I saw a coupon in the Sunday paper for a round-trip flight from Dallas to London for $447. It's on Atlas Air but I wanted to check your best fare because I'm a frequent flyer with Global Village and I'd like to get the miles for the trip.

FRIENDLY FRAN: I'm glad you called us, and I'll be happy to check our lowest fare to London. That's a lot of miles! When are you planning to travel?

TRAVELIN' TRAVIS: In April, around the 15th.

FRIENDLY FRAN: What a nice time to go to London! Well, if you leave on a Sunday, Monday, or Tuesday—that would be the 16th, 17th, or 18th—and return on one of those days as well, we can get you a direct flight to Heathrow airport for $515 round-trip. That's our Spring Special fare. Would you like me to make you a reservation? We can hold it at no obligation for 24 hours. That gives you some time to think about what will work best for you.

TRAVELIN' TRAVIS: $515, huh? That's quite a bit more than Atlas's fare, but I *would* like to take a direct flight. Sure, go ahead and reserve a space for me. The name's Jones—Travis Jones.

FRIENDLY FRAN: Great, I hope this works for you. I can book you on the morning flight, which would put you into London in the early evening, or you can take the night flight and arrive at 8 a.m. Which would you prefer, Mr. Jones?

Techniques for Building Rapport

All customer service representatives have the opportunity to build rapport in every interaction with the customer. Although there's no "right" formula for building rapport, there are a few simple techniques that can be helpful:

1. Use the customer's name.

2. Say "please" and "thank you."

3. Explain your reasons for saying no.

4. Show your interest in the customer's needs.

5. Be empathetic to the customer's feelings.

6. Let the customer know his or her options.

6

Stop, Look, and Listen

Games for Focusing on the Customer's Needs

Amateur Architects

In a Nutshell

This is a lengthy but popular game in which participants learn to use open and closed questions strategically. Their objective is to draw a house as described by their partners. This game is excellent for helping both new and experienced employees improve their questioning skills.

Time

30–40 minutes.

What You'll Need

Overhead transparencies or flip-charts of the information on pages 114 and 115. One copy of the "House A" hand-out on page 116 for half the participants, one copy of the "House B" handout on page 117 for half the participants. Blank paper and pens or pencils.

What to Do

Use the information on pages 114 and 115 to explain the difference between open and closed questions.

Put participants into pairs and explain that the object of the game is for one participant to draw a house that matches the house his or her partner will be given. Participants who are drawing can ask any questions they want and as many as they want in five minutes. Participants who are describing the house should follow the instructions on the handout.

Distribute the "House A" handout to the participants who will be describing the house; hand out a sheet of blank paper to the participants who will be drawing. Ask partners to sit back-to-back and spread participants out so that those drawing cannot see the houses of those who are describing.

After five minutes, have the describer and drawer compare houses. Debrief the game. Point out how open questions tend to solicit more general information than closed questions.

Have pairs switch roles. Distribute the "House B" handout to the participants who will be describing the house; hand out a blank sheet of paper to the participants who will be drawing.

After five minutes, have the describer and drawer compare houses and debrief the game.

Discussion Questions

Q: What type of questions work best when you need to gather information?

A: *A combination. Open questions get more information to start with, but when you need specifics, you need to use closed questions.*

If You Have More Time

Develop a list of open and closed questions participants can use to gather information from their customers to help them better understand and meet customer needs.

Open Questions

- Solicit more than a "yes" or "no" or other one-word response.

- Aim to get someone talking.

- Are useful when you want general information.

- Common lead-ins are what, how, and why.

Closed Questions

- Solicit a "yes" or "no" or other one-word response.

- Aim to limit talking or to control direction of conversation.

- Are useful when you want specific information.

- Common lead-ins are who, when, did, which, would, are, can, have, do, is, will, and may.

House "A"

Answer questions about the house as asked. If your partner asks you an open question, describe several features about the house. If your partner asks a closed question, only give a "yes," "no," or short reply. Do not volunteer information.

House "B"

Answer questions about the house as asked. If your partner asks you an open question, describe several features about the house. If your partner asks a closed question, only give a "yes," "no," or short reply. Do not volunteer information.

Listen Up!

In a Nutshell

In this activity, participants assess their own listening skills. This activity is appropriate for introducing listening skills training for inexperienced employees. It is also appropriate as a self-check to remind seasoned employees of the importance of listening to the customer and as a way to identify areas for improvement.

Time

5–10 minutes.

What You'll Need

One copy of the handouts on pages 120 and 121 for each participant.

What to Do

Give the two handouts to each participant. Give them five minutes to complete the assessments.

Ask participants to select one aspect of listening that they will focus on during the following week.

Listen Up!

Some people are good listeners while others are not. Most of us fall some-where in the middle—we're good listeners in some situations, with some peo-ple, when discussing some topics. Take a moment now to evaluate your listen-ing skills. How do you believe the following people would rate you—on a scale of 1 to 5—as a listener? (5 = best)

Yourself   _____

Your customers   _____

Your boss   _____

Your co-workers   _____

Your best friend _____

Now add the scores together and plot the total on the listening spectrum.

5	10	15	20	25

Brick Wall . . . .*The Human Ear*

120

Listen Up!

Review the following list of poor listening habits and mark each with an "F" (frequently), "S" (sometimes), or "R" (rarely) according to how often you exhibit the tendency:

_____ I pretend I'm paying attention when my mind is drifting off.

_____ I cut people off or finish their sentences because I know what they're going to say.

_____ When someone is speaking to me, I look around the room to see what else is happening.

_____ I shuffle papers on my desk or start doing some other task when someone talks too long or too slowly.

_____ When someone is speaking, I plan what I will say next.

_____ When a person speaks too fast or uses words I don't understand, I let it go and listen only for what I do understand.

What can you do during the upcoming week to improve your listening skills?

_____

_____

_____

Barriers to Listening

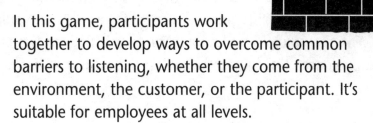

In a Nutshell

In this game, participants work together to develop ways to overcome common barriers to listening, whether they come from the environment, the customer, or the participant. It's suitable for employees at all levels.

Time

15–20 minutes.

What You'll Need

One copy of the handouts on pages 124 and 125 for each group of participants.

What to Do

Distribute the handout and ask participants to work in groups of three or four to identify ways to overcome these common listening barriers.

Listening Barriers

Being a good listener means identifying and overcoming barriers. Review the following barriers to listening, and consider what you would do to overcome them. For example, if you had a poor connection on the telephone, you would overcome this barrier by calling the customer back.

Noisy work space _____

_____

_____

Visual distractions _____

_____

_____

Tiredness _____

_____

_____

Customer speaks too fast or has an accent _____

_____

_____

(Page 2)

Customer speaks too slowly or too much _____

_____

_____

Communication is unclear, poorly organized, or includes unfamiliar terms ____

_____

_____

_____

Expectations about the communication (for example, you think you know
what the other person is going to say) _____

_____

_____

_____

Stress or mental restlessness _____

_____

_____

Customer uses emotionally charged words or statements _____

_____

_____

Pass It Along

In a Nutshell

This game is a variation of the "Telephone" game everyone has played at one time or another. The twist is that participants play the game twice, the second time using confirming statements to echo what they've heard before passing it along. This activity highlights the importance of confirming information given by customers, which in turn eliminates errors and increases customer satisfaction. It is an ideal game for anyone who has to interpret or give complex information.

Time

10–15 minutes.

What You'll Need

Before the activity, make one copy of the "messages" on page 130 for each group of participants. Cut each copy so that you have four pieces of paper, each with one message written on it.

You'll also need a copy of Confirming Your Understanding (page 131) on an overhead, flip-chart, or white board.

What to Do

Divide participants into groups of four to five persons and have each group sit in a small circle, facing one another. Tell participants that they will verbally relay a message to their co-workers. Read the following rules to participants:

1. You can only say the message once.

2. You must whisper the message into the ear of the person sitting on your left. No one else in the group should be able to hear the message until it has been whispered in their ear.

3. Once you've heard the message, you should repeat it exactly as you've understood it.

4. The last person in the group to hear the message should say it out loud so the group can compare it with the original message.

Choose one member of each group to start, and give that person one of the slips of paper. All groups should get the same message during each round.

Each group should play two rounds of the game (with different messages) before moving on to the next stage. After they've played two rounds, briefly go over Confirming Your Understanding and solicit volunteers to give a few examples of confirming.

Tell the groups to play two more rounds of the game, using the two remaining messages. This time, each participant should use a confirming statement to make sure he or she got the message right before passing it along.

During this stage, the game gets a little more complicated. Participants should follow these rules:

1. Give the message as if you were the customer, using an "I..." statement.

2. When you confirm, follow the steps, using a "You..." statement. Then pass the message exactly as you heard it ("I....").

Participants should whisper the confirming statement into the ear of the person who gave them the message. Once they've confirmed they got it right, they should pass it along.

Discussion Questions

Q: What differences did you notice when you used confirming statements?

A: *A higher level of accuracy.*

Q: Is it necessary to confirm every request from customers?

A: *No. Simple, straightforward requests don't require confirming.*

Q: Why should you confirm your understanding before carrying out the customer's request?

A: *It assures fewer errors and shows customers you're concerned about getting it right. It also gives customers a chance to make sure they said what they intended to say.*

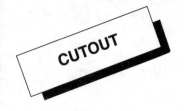

Message One

I'm going on vacation from July 2 to August 4 and I'd like to stop delivery of the paper during that time. I also want to arrange for early delivery of the Sunday paper; I think you have an arrangement in which you can get the Sunday paper on Saturday evening.

Message Two

I want to change my individual account to a joint one, and I'd like some information on your new arrangements for small business loans. What kind of rate do you offer for a short-term, sub-ten thousand dollar loan?

Message Three

I'm interested in bringing a group to the museum on July 6. There will be ten children, three senior citizens, and four adults over eighteen, but one's a student. Would it be better to go with your senior and student discounts or with a group rate?

Message Four

I want to order two dozen roses, but they'll be going to two different addresses. One's for my mother in Oakland and the other is for my sister in Orinda. I want to make sure they're very fresh—sweetheart roses for my mom and sterling silvers for my sister.

Confirming Your Understanding

Step 1   **Use a confirming statement.**

> Let me confirm...
> Let me make sure I understand your request...
> So you want...
> I'd just like to confirm that...

Step 2   **Summarize key facts.**

> You want to compare benefits for hospital stays.
> You'd like to find out if floor seats are available.
> Your shipment never arrived.

Step 3   **Ask if your understanding is correct.**

> Did I get that right?
> Is that correct?
> Did I understand you correctly?
> Right?
> Is that it?

Step 4   **Clarify misunderstandings (if necessary).**

Say What?

In a Nutshell

This activity teaches participants to confirm their understanding of a customer's statement or request. It is a good activity to use if your employees frequently act without thoroughly understanding the customer's situation.

Time

10–15 minutes.

What You'll Need

One copy of the handout on page 131 for each participant. Blank paper for taking notes.

What to Do

Review the steps for confirming understanding from the handout on page 131.

Hand out a blank sheet of paper to each participant. Tell them that you will be reading some customer statements. Their job is to take notes of the key facts they hear and then use the four steps of confirming listed on the handout to confirm their understanding of your statement. When they have a confirming statement ready, they should stand up.

Read the following statements and ask the first few participants who stand up to read their confirming statements. Reward them with candy or other small prizes.

1. I'm interested in bringing a group to the zoo on April 10. There will be ten children, four adults over eighteen, and four senior citizens. Two of the adults are students. Do you have special discounts for students and senior citizens? Or a group discount?

2. I got some of your software for Christmas and it doesn't work. Well, it works, but now my computer clock doesn't work and I'm missing appointments. I don't know what I should do.

3. I lived in Ohio until the end of October, when I retired. I came here to California to live with my son because of the weather and my asthma. The doctor here took me off my medicine and my asthma has improved a lot. So I sent the bill that I paid back to Ohio. They sent it back and told me to send it to you in California. So I need to know where to send it, and then I need to know if I need a new ID card since I moved. I really am feeling a lot better, but I need to know if there will be any changes to my policy next year.

4. I've had a checking account and a savings account with your bank for the past few years. I've just turned 55, and now I don't know if I'm supposed to be in the Senior Gold Account or if I should stay in the standard account. Actually, my wife said we might be better off. We don't have many checks we write each month.

5. I want to take two classes at your South County campus: "How to Start Your Own Business" and "Ten Weeks to Better Parenting." When do I come?

Have participants post a copy of the overhead near their desks until they have mastered this skill.

If You Have More Time

Put participants in pairs. One participant will develop a complex statement that would be heard on the job; the other participant will practice confirming his or her understanding. Then have them switch roles and do it again.

7

The Sky's the Limit

Creative Ways to Customize Your Service

If I Could Do Anything

In a Nutshell

Pairs compete in a mock contest to come up with ideas for promoting their products and delighting their customers. This game aims to get participants thinking creatively about the many ways to serve customers and the connection between happy customers and profitable business. The contest works best with six to eight pairs and is suitable for all service employees.

Time

15–20 minutes.

What You'll Need

Make one copy of the fictional businesses on pages 141 and 142. Cut the sheets so that you have several slips of paper, each with one business on it. You'll also need a hat, bowl, or basket in which to put the slips of paper so that the participants can randomly draw them.

What to Do

Tell the group that they'll be participating in a Creative Service Contest sponsored by the local community business association. They'll be given a fictional business to represent and they'll work in pairs to come up with an idea for the contest.

The purpose of the contest is to come up with an idea that will both promote the business and offer something special to customers. Encourage participants to be as creative as possible in coming up with their ideas. There are no budgetary restrictions, but entries must be "reasonable." The ideas should relate to the business; for example, a grocery store couldn't offer free puppies.

Share the following sample entry with the participants to give them an idea of how the game works.

Name of company: Millennium Bank
Line of business: Bank
Idea: We're going to give free checking for life to every 2000th person who signs up for a Millennium checking or savings account.

Assign pairs and ask one representative from each pair to pick a slip of paper from the "hat." Give participants about ten minutes to come up with their ideas, and then go around the room and have each pair announce their business and their idea. Then take a vote to see who wins the contest.

If You Have More Time

After the activity, you can ask pairs to come up with creative ideas for promoting their own product or service to customers.

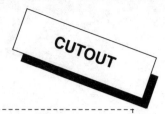

Name of company: **The Game of Life**

Line of business: **Sporting goods store**

Idea: _____

_____

_____

Name of company: **Quo Vadis?**

Line of business: **Shuttle service**

Idea: _____

_____

_____

Name of company: **A Tree Fell**

Line of business: **Woodworking shop**

Idea: _____

_____

_____

Name of company: **Beauty and the Beast**

Line of business: **Unisex barber shop**

Idea: _____

_____

_____

Name of company: **Call on Me**

Line of business: **Cellular phone service**

Idea: _____

_____

_____

Name of company: **Page One**

Line of business: **Bookstore**

Idea: _____

_____

_____

Name of company: **The Daisy Chain**

Line of business: **Florist**

Idea: _____

_____

_____

Name of company: **The City Zoo**

Line of business: **One of the country's largest zoos**

Idea: _____

_____

_____

The Great Service Debate

In a Nutshell

This is a lively game in which the group is divided into two teams which must debate each other to determine the best solution to a difficult customer service situation. It's best suited to employees who can be trusted to have an intelligent, professional debate.

Time

15–20 minutes.

What You'll Need

Two copies of the handout on page 145. Participants will need paper and pens. You will need a flip-chart and markers.

What to Do

Divide the group into two teams of equal size. Tell them they will review a customer service scenario and will then hold a debate to determine what course of action should be taken by the customer service representative.

Give each team a copy of the handout and assign each team a position to defend. Give them a few minutes to discuss their position and to elect a spokesperson. Then hold the debate.

As the debate takes place, you can write the "pros" of each side's position on a flip-chart or white board divided into two columns. The objective of this debate is not for one side to win but for the group to examine and discuss a diverse variety of customer service issues.

Discussion Questions

Q: What did you learn from the debate?

Q: How many of you represented a position that you would not have taken if given a choice?

Q: How would a similar situation be resolved if it took place here at our organization?

If You Have More Time

Hold a second debate, this time focusing on a customer service situation that the participants might face in their own jobs.

*Y*ou work at Wanamaker Widget Factory as a customer service representative. Your company is currently facing a widget shortage and has put a temporary limit on widget sales: 2000 widgets per customer per week. One day you take a call from Alvin Zinger at South Coast Supplies. He's a longtime customer who usually orders about 4000 widgets per week. When you tell Alvin about the temporary limit on widget sales, he informs you that he'll either get 4000 widgets a week from you or he'll buy 4000 widgets from your competitor, Walla Walla Widget Factory. Argue for your team's position, regardless of what you might do if you actually faced the situation in your own job.

Team A: Your position is that the factory should make an exception for Mr. Zinger and agree to sell him 4000 widgets per week.

Team B: Your position is that Mr. Zinger should not receive more than the allotted quota of widgets.

Rules for Debate

1. All members of your team should participate in the team discussion.

2. Designate one spokesperson to argue your position.

3. You will have five minutes to discuss your position and come up with a list of reasons to support it. Then you will have two minutes to speak about why your team's course of action is the best one.

4. After each side has spoken, your team will have two minutes to come up with rebuttals to your opponents' argument. You'll then have one minute to voice your rebuttal, and the debate ends.

Service Spoken Here

In a Nutshell

In this activity, participants brainstorm creative ideas for serving their customers. This activity is best used after participants understand the meaning of customer service.

Time

10–15 minutes.

What You'll Need

A flip-chart or white board and marker pen. Blank paper.

What to Do

Put participants in groups of three or four. Tell groups to imagine that they made the rules regarding what could be done for your customers. Ask them what measures—small or large—they might take to serve their customers better.

Tell them to be specific; for example, rather than say, "I wouldn't make them wait on hold so long," they should say, "I'd guarantee a hold-time of no more than two minutes."

Give each group a blank sheet of paper to record their thoughts.

After five minutes, ask each group to report on the results of their brainstorming. List answers on a flip-chart or white board.

Determine which ideas can be implemented right away and ask participants to put them into practice. For those ideas that require further research and/or management's approval, make a list to review with management. Be sure to let participants know the outcome.

I Wanna Be Me

In a Nutshell

In this activity, participants examine their own preferences for business interactions and compare them with the preferences of their customers. The objective of the activity is for participants to learn that it is easy to customize service to customers. This activity is suitable for service employees at all levels.

Time

20–30 minutes.

What You'll Need

One copy of the overhead on page 151. One copy of the handout on page 152 for each participant.

What to Do

Review the overhead. Explain that some people are more relationship-oriented and some people are more task-oriented; some people prefer to get to know people by socializing with them and others prefer to get to know people by working on a project with them. Ask participants to make a mental mark on the y axis as to where they fall in this continuum.

Then explain that some people are fast-paced and others are slow-paced; some people move quickly, speak quickly, and make decisions quickly, whereas others move and speak more slowly and are more analytical or cautious in making a decision. Ask participants to make a mental mark on the x axis as to where they fall on this continuum. Then have participants put themselves into one quadrant, based on their two marks.

Ask them to consider someone they get along with very well and determine which quadrant that person belongs to; then have them do the same with someone they find difficult. Discuss the results.

Distribute the handout and give participants a few moments to review it. Explain that there is no right or wrong quadrant; each quadrant has its positive and negative aspects. Point out that the problem arises when a person from one quadrant enters a business transaction with a person from another quadrant, particularly if the people are in diametrically opposed quadrants.

For example, a Q1 customer may feel like a Q3 service representative is not listening and is abrupt and possibly rude—just because the Q3 representative gets right down to business and asks rapid-fire questions.

Ask participants to think about five of their customers and decide how they might change the way they interact with those customers in order to offer more customized service.

Relationship-oriented

**Fast-
paced**

Task-oriented

Relationship-oriented

Q1

- Likes to talk about family, friends, activities, and other personal information
- Appreciates you taking time to develop a personal relationship or a business "friendship"
- Likes to be given information verbally—preferably face-to-face
- Doesn't like to be pushed into making quick decisions

Q2

- Likes to tell stories based on personal experience
- Will take time to develop a personal relationship or a business "friendship" with you
- Doesn't want a lot of detail—just key facts
- Tends to make decisions quickly based in large part on personal relationships

Slow-paced

Fast-paced

Q4

- Prefers talking about the business situation at hand rather than making small talk
- Likes to have lots of back-up data
- Doesn't like to be pushed into making quick decisions
- Tends to analyze all the details before making a decision

Q3

- Wants to get down to business quickly
- Is more interested in getting the job done than in becoming your friend
- May ask lots of questions; you feel like you're being "grilled"
- Tends to make decisions quickly based on the facts—likes written summaries of key points

Task-oriented

Make It Personal

In a Nutshell

This game serves as a gimmick to make participants realize that there are literally hundreds of ways they can offer good service to customers. Each participant uses the letters of his or her name to inspire service-oriented actions. It's a fun activity to use as an energizing "filler" or as a warm-up to a more intensive customer service training session.

Time

10 minutes.

What You'll Need

Each participant will need a piece of paper and a pen. You'll need a flip-chart or white board and markers.

What to Do

Tell each participant to write his or her name vertically along the center of a sheet of paper. Demonstrate by writing the following on a flip-chart or white board:

M
A
R
Y

Tell participants that now their task is to use each letter of their name to come up with an action that they can take to offer great service to their customers. Each letter of their name must begin a word in the action phrase, but it doesn't necessarily have to be the first word of the phrase. Actions can be phrased either positively or negatively. For example:

Be **M**otivated to serve.
   Ask if there's anything else I can do for them.
   Respect their needs.
Don't **Y**odel in the customer's presence.

Encourage participants to have fun with this activity and to be as creative as possible. Almost anything goes!

After seven or eight minutes, ask for some volunteers to share what they came up with. Point out to participants that there are hundreds, even thousands of ways to give great service to their customers.

Tip! If the participants like what they came up with, they can post it at their work station.

8

When the Going Gets Tough

Games for Dealing with Difficult Customers

Bill of Rights

In a Nutshell

In this game, participants work together to brainstorm the special needs of upset and dissatisfied customers. The objective is to create a Bill of Rights for these customers. This game is suitable for all employees who deal with upset and dissatisfied customers.

Time

15 minutes.

What You'll Need

Participants will need pen and paper. You'll need a flip-chart or white board and markers.

What to Do

Remind participants that there are many reasons why a customer might be upset, but no matter what the reason, the attitude and skills of the employee are of paramount importance in turning around the situation. Studies have shown that if upset customers are treated fairly, they're likely to continue doing business with the company.

Customers who are unhappy with a service or product have the same needs as other customers—empathy, respect, courtesy, etc.—but they need some extra special treatment as well. Tell participants that in this game they're going to brainstorm the special needs of customers who are upset or dissatisfied with a service or product your company provides. Think of it as a Bill of Rights for dissatisfied customers.

Divide participants into groups of two or three and ask them to discuss their own experiences with upset customers and brainstorm some ideas for the Bill of Rights. After about ten minutes, ask groups what ideas they came up with, and capture these on a flip-chart or white board. Answers will vary, but be sure the participants hit upon the following needs of upset customers:

- To be taken seriously
- To be listened to and understood
- To be respected, not condescended to
- To receive immediate action
- To be assured that a problem won't happen again

Remind participants that these courtesies can be extended to customers through their tone of voice, actions, and overall attitude.

Tip! You may want to create a professional-looking version of the "Upset Customers' Bill of Rights" for participants to post in their work areas.

Service Means Not Always Having to Say You're Sorry

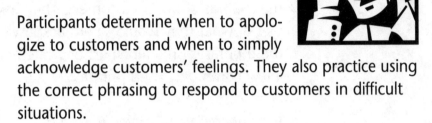

In a Nutshell

Participants determine when to apologize to customers and when to simply acknowledge customers' feelings. They also practice using the correct phrasing to respond to customers in difficult situations.

This game sets forward the policy that it's not necessary to automatically apologize to upset or disgruntled customers. If your organization's policy differs, this may not be an ideal game for your group.

Time

15–20 minutes.

What You'll Need

A few pieces of red and green construction paper or poster board, cut into pieces about the size of an index card. Each participant will need one red and one green card. A flip-chart and markers.

What to Do

Tell participants that they're going to practice two skills that are an integral part of the customer service role, particularly when dealing with upset or disgruntled customers. They're going to practice acknowledging customers' feelings and apologizing to customers when the organization is at fault.

Ask participants why it's important to acknowledge the feelings of upset customers. Then ask for some examples of what they would say to acknowledge. Capture these phrases on a flip-chart or white board. Following are a few commonly used phrases:

I can appreciate what you're saying.
I can see how you'd be upset.
I would be upset too.
I can hear that you're annoyed.
I understand your concern.

Then ask participants when they feel it's necessary to apologize to customers. Conventional wisdom says that you should apologize when you or your organization is at fault, but not when the customer is upset for some other reason. For example, if a customer ordered the wrong size dress, you wouldn't have to apologize; but if the customer ordered the right size and the company sent the wrong size, then you should apologize.

Ask for some examples of how the participants would apologize to customers. Capture these on another page of the flip-chart.

Following are some standard apologies:

I apologize for the error.
I'm sorry.
We're sorry for the mix-up.
We were wrong.

Now hand out the green and red cards and tell the participants that you'll read out some customer statements and they will raise either a red or a green card. Red means apologize; green means acknowledge only. Mention to participants that usually an apology includes an acknowledgment.

Read out each customer statement on page 162 and tell the participants to raise their cards. After each statement, choose one participant to give an example of the acknowledging statement or apology she or he would use in this situation.

Note: There may be some disagreement as to what participants would do in some situations. This is natural; there are no absolutely right or wrong answers. If participants are divided, ask for an example of both an acknowledgment and an apology.

If You Have More Time

Ask for some common customer complaints that the participants receive and have them come up with acknowledging statements and apologies, as appropriate.

Statements from Dissatisfied Customers

1. I've been transferred several times; I think you people are giving me the runaround.

   I can hear that you're annoyed. What can I do for you today?

2. I just spoke to a young man who was very flip with me when I told him about my problem with the jeweled dog collar I ordered.

   I'm sorry you were treated that way and I can understand why you'd be upset.

3. Well, I just assumed your company had a money-back guarantee. Nobody told me that you didn't.

   I can tell you're upset, Mrs. Jamison.

4. I've been waiting five weeks for my directory to arrive, and when I first called, I was told I would receive it within ten days.

   I apologize for the delay; I know it must be frustrating for you.

5. Your prices are too high for me! I'm retired and on a limited income.

   I can sure appreciate your need to save money.

6. My briefcase arrived with the wrong monogram!

   Oh no! I'm sorry for the mistake.

7. This bill says that my emergency room visit cost $700. I was only there for an hour!

   I understand your concern. Medical costs are frequently quite high.

8. I want to return this software. My computer doesn't have enough space on my hard drive for it.

   That must be disappointing.

The Problem Tree

In a Nutshell

In this game, participants work together to identify and prioritize the challenges they face on the job. It's a useful game for airing grievances and for identifying the problems faced by your employees. This game is suitable for all employees.

Time

10–15 minutes.

What You'll Need

Draw a large tree on a flip-chart or white board. Using colored construction paper, cut out several red apples, yellow pears, and orange oranges. (Each "fruit" should be approximately three inches in diameter.) You'll also need masking tape.

What to Do

Divide participants into groups of three or four and give each group a few of each fruit. Ask them to discuss the various challenges they face as customer service employees and to select three challenges. They should then choose a fruit on which to describe each challenge. Apples are for critical challenges, oranges are for significant challenges, and pears are for minor challenges. They can use whatever fruit they want, but they cannot describe more than three challenges. Give participants about five minutes to do this. Then have them tape the fruits on the tree.

Next, read the challenges out loud and use a blank piece of flip-chart paper to list the challenges in order of priority (apples first, then oranges, then pears). If one challenge has been given different priorities, list it under the more critical ranking. Ask the participants if the list accurately reflects their view of how the department's challenges should be prioritized.

Note: The objective of this game is to identify challenges; the next step is to put together a plan for overcoming them. Be sure to let participants know how you plan to address the problems they've identified.

Down the Stairs

In a Nutshell

Participants work together to come up with ideas for preventing minor challenges from escalating. The objective is to move a figure down the staircase by addressing the challenges represented on each step. This game is helpful for anyone who regularly faces challenges—both simple and complex—in their interactions with customers.

Time

10 minutes.

What You'll Need

Draw a staircase with seven steps on it (side view) on a flip-chart or white board. Using colored paper or cardstock, cut out the figure of a person and put the figure on the top step of the staircase. (Use a piece of masking tape on the back so that the figure can easily be moved down the staircase.)

What to Do

Divide the participants into pairs or small groups and tell them the objective of this game is to quickly come up with solutions to common challenges in the customer service environment. At each step, they'll be asked how they would respond to a potentially challenging customer service situation. If their answers are acceptable, the figure will move down to the next step.

Begin the game by announcing the first challenge and asking participants what they would do to prevent the challenge from escalating. Give them a few moments to confer with their partners and then ask for answers. This should be a fast-paced, lively game.

Answers will vary and they don't have to be identical to those below, but you must get at least one acceptable answer before you move the figure down to the next step. Continue until participants have addressed all seven challenges.

Reward participants with candy or another small treat.

Following are the challenges that correspond to each step and some possible responses:

1. You don't know the answer to the customer's question.

   Let the customer know that you don't know the answer; ask your manager or supervisor.

2. You have to say no to the customer's request.

   Apologize, if appropriate, and tell the customer what you can do. Explain your reasons for saying no.

3. Your computer is moving slowly and the customer is getting impatient.

   Tell the customer your computer is moving slowly; use transition statements to avoid long periods of silence.

4. The customer has unreasonable expectations.

   Emphasize what you can do for the customer.

5. The customer is skeptical about what you're telling him.

   Offer to show him proof or documentation; ask a manager or supervisor to confirm what you've told the customer.

6. The customer is angry for no apparent reason.

   Speak in a calm voice; acknowledge the customer's feelings.

7. The customer refuses to give you all the information you need.

   Explain why you need the information and then ask the customer to reconsider giving it to you.

If You Have More Time

Play the game again with challenges you've prepared ahead of time based on situations the participants commonly face.

Stress Buster Cards

In a Nutshell

Participants create a job aid they can use to eliminate stress and maintain their poise when facing challenging customers or customer service situations. It's suitable for any employees who work in stressful environments.

Time

5–10 minutes.

What You'll Need

Several large index cards (one for each participant, plus some extras) and a set of multicolored drawing pens.

What to Do

Hold a brief discussion about ways to overcome the stress that occurs when a customer service situation turns challenging. Remind participants that simple, natural techniques such as visualization, deep breathing, and even smiling have been proven to have a calming and reenergizing effect on stressed individuals.

Pass out the index cards and tell participants to write their own stress-busting techniques on the card. They can write anything they like, and they may want to include three or four stress busters on the card. Following are a few suggestions: a favorite quote, a cherished memory, the name of a loved one, a mantra or visualization, the punchline of a favorite joke, a description of a previous challenge he or she handled well.

Let participants choose some colored pens to illustrate their Stress Buster Cards however they wish. Tell them to keep the cards in their work stations so that they're always accessible when needed.

Wait! That's Not All

Techniques to Up-sell and Cross-sell
for Ultimate Customer Satisfaction

Is There Anything Else?

In a Nutshell

In this activity, participants brainstorm creative ways to uncover additional needs and to avoid the trite phrase, "Is there anything else I can help you with today?" This activity is ideal for employees who manage lengthy or complex customer interactions or those who need to uncover additional customer requests for service.

Time

5–10 minutes.

What You'll Need

Blank sheets of flip-chart paper and markers. One blank sheet of paper per participant.

What to Do

Point out that it's always a good idea to ask customers if there is something else you can help them with before closing out the interaction. However, the phrase "Is there anything else?" is trite and overused. There are many other ways to uncover additional service opportunities.

Ask participants to work in groups of three to four to brainstorm additional ways to uncover requests for service. Give each group a blank piece of flip-chart paper and a marker pen and ask them to record their answers.

After five minutes, ask each group to present their responses.

Answers

Here are some possible phrases to use:

- What else can I do for you today?
- How else can I be of service?
- What else might you be looking for?
- What else prompted your call/visit today?
- Do you have any other questions I can answer for you?
- What else can I help you with today?

It's Not Just a Fruit

In a Nutshell

In this game, participants learn to cross-sell or substitute-sell by outlining the features and benefits of common "products" such as a banana. The game is useful for anyone who needs to describe or sell a product or service to a customer.

Time

10 minutes.

What You'll Need

An overhead transparency or flip-chart with the information on page 177. Blank flip-chart paper and marker pens.

What to Do

Using the overhead transparency, discuss the concepts of features and benefits. Remind participants that customers buy benefits, not features, and that pointing out benefits is particularly important when trying to cross-sell or substitute-sell.

Put participants into groups of three to five. Explain that their job is to work together to develop a list of features and benefits for some common "products."

Assign one product from the following list to each group.

- A banana
- A safety pin
- A lollipop
- A cat
- A rose
- A chocolate-chip cookie

Hand out a piece of blank flip-chart paper and a pen to each group. Ask participants to list the features of their product and then to list the corresponding benefits. One way to find benefits is to ask, "So what?" For example: "Our sunscreen has an SPF of 15." "So what?" "So you can stay in the sun longer without burning."

After four or five minutes, ask each group to present the features and benefits of their product. Ask "So what?" after each feature until the group agrees that a compelling benefit has been presented.

If You Have More Time

Have each group develop a feature and benefit chart for one of their company's products. After presentations have been made, type up the feature and benefit information and distribute it for use on the job.

Features and Benefits

A **feature** is a distinct part or quality of a product or service.

"Our sun block has an SPF of 15."

A **benefit** is the value of the feature to the customer.

"This means you can sit out in the sun longer without burning."

Product Partners

In a Nutshell

Participants are assigned products to represent and they mingle with one another to establish as many "partnerships" as they can, based on a commonality between their two products. This game reinforces creative thinking and the ability to establish relationships between diverse objects. It's ideal for employees who need to cross-sell.

Time

10–15 minutes.

What You'll Need

One copy of the product list on page 182. A hat, bag, or basket. Participants will also need paper and pens and may want a clipboard or other hard surface for writing.

What to Do

Cut the copy of the product list from page 182 into pieces so that you have 16 slips of paper, each with the name of one product. Put these in a hat or basket.

Tell participants they'll select a product to represent and then they will go around the room to talk to other participants to try to establish partnerships based on a commonality between their products. The objective is to create as many partnerships as they can in the allotted time.

For example, someone who sells oranges might be able to create a partnership with someone who sells apples because they both sell fruit. The same person could create a partnership with someone who sells balls because their respective products are both round.

Participants should work with one another to establish relationships between their products, but they should not spend more than one or two minutes with each potential partner. None of the participants will be able to establish partnerships with everyone they talk to. Each time they establish a partnership, they should record their partner and the product relationship on a piece of paper.

Once you've explained the game, ask participants to draw a product from the "hat" and begin the game. After about ten minutes, stop the game and ask for volunteers to share their results.

Trainer Note: Countless combinations are possible. Following are just a few:

1. Things people use at work (telephone, books, paper, computer, cardboard boxes, eyeglasses)

2. Things people like to receive as gifts (flowers, clothing, chocolates, music tapes, and CDs)

3. Things people put on their coffee table at home (flowers, books)

4. Things people use to communicate (telephones, computers, pens, paper, musical instruments)

5. Things almost everyone owns (telephone, cars, books, shoes, televisions)

6. Things you pay tax on (everything)

7. Things that die (flowers, cars)

If You Have More Time

Ask participants to work in small groups to develop "product partners" for their products and services.

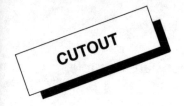

CUTOUT

Product List

You sell books.	You sell paper.
You sell telephones.	You sell shoes.
You sell computer equipment.	You sell musical instruments.
You sell pens and pencils.	You sell cardboard boxes.
You sell flowers.	You sell eyeglasses.
You sell chocolates.	You sell furniture.
You sell clothing.	You sell cars.
You sell sporting goods.	You sell televisions.

And by the Way . . .

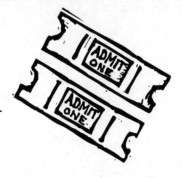

In a Nutshell

Participants learn when and how to up-sell when talking with customers. This game is ideal for employees who have the opportunity to increase order value through using these techniques.

Time

5–10 minutes.

What You'll Need

One copy of the handout on page 185 for each participant. One copy of page 186 for every four participants. A hat, box, or basket.

What to Do

Distribute and review the handout on page 185. Tell participants that they are going to work in pairs to practice up-selling.

Cut the copies of page 186 into individual scenarios and place them in a hat, box, or basket. Arrange participants into pairs and have each pair draw one scenario. The pairs are to work together to develop an up-selling statement. For example, assume the scenario drawn says, "The customer orders a gross of pencils. See if the customer is interested in saving $0.05 per pencil by ordering two gross." In this case, the statement might be, "That was 144 pencils at $0.65 each. You know, Elliot, I can lower your price by $0.05 per pencil if you order two gross. Would that work for you?"

Give participants two to three minutes to develop their statements, then have each pair share its statement with the class. Offer candy or other small reward to each pair.

If You Have More Time

Have participants do the exercise again, this time with product scenarios from your own company that you have prepared in advance.

Up-selling

When you up-sell, you increase the value of an order by asking the customer to commit to a higher quantity. This is typically done when customers can obtain a price break or another perk if they purchase at a higher quantity. When up-selling, always include a benefit to the customer (we've underlined the benefit to show you what we mean). Up-selling sounds like this:

Mr. Smith, I can <u>drop that price for you by $2.48</u> on each unit if you can increase your order by two cases. Does that make sense for you?

John, we're having a special offer this week that will help you <u>lower your cost</u>. I can offer you 25% off if you order at least 100. Would you like to do that?

I saw you looking at that great travel mug. You know, if you purchase $45 worth of merchandise today, you can get one of those mugs <u>free</u>! Can I show you some of our line?

The steps for up-selling are as follows:

1. Explain how the customer can save money by increasing the order. Be sure to include a benefit to the customer.

2. Ask the customer to commit to a larger order.

Up-selling

Scenario One

Josh Foster bought a ticket to the theater for Sunday night for $45. See if Josh would be interested in purchasing two tickets and saving $10 off the ticket price of each ticket.

Scenario Two

You work in a clothing shop. A customer is just about to purchase two pairs of socks for $4.99 a pair. The store currently has a special of five pairs for $19.99. See if the customer would be interested in increasing the number of pairs in order to save money.

Scenario Three

You work in a computer store and you've been answering questions for Jim about your lowest priced computer. It seems as if price is very important to Jim, but you know that a computer that costs $150 more also includes three software packages that might be useful. This upgrade would save Jim $650 over the price of the lower priced computer plus the software. See if Jim is interested in this upgrade.

Scenario Four

You sell tickets at a movie theater. A customer that you see on a regular basis is in line. You can offer this customer a "book" of 10 tickets that will save the customer 10% off the cost of individual admissions. When the customer approaches the window, see if she would be interested in purchasing the ticket book.

Would You Like Fries with Your Burger?

In a Nutshell

Participants learn when and how to cross-sell when talking with customers. This game is ideal for employees who have the opportunity to increase order value through using these techniques.

Time

5–10 minutes.

What You'll Need

One copy of the handout on page 189 for each participant. One copy of page 190 for every eight participants. A hat, box, or basket.

What to Do

Distribute and review the handout on page 189. Tell participants that they are going to work in groups of two to practice cross-selling.

Cut the copies of page 190 into individual scenarios and place them in a hat, box, or basket. Arrange participants into pairs and have each pair draw one scenario. The pairs are to work together to develop a cross-selling statement. For example, assume the scenario said, "The customer orders a top hat. See if the customer is also interested in gloves or a cane." In this case, the statement might be, "By the way, Mr. Astaire, we also have some high-quality gloves and a very handsome cane that would look smashing with your top hat. Would you like me to tell you more about them?"

Give participants two to three minutes to develop their statements; then have each group share their statement out loud.

If You Have More Time

Have participants play the game again, this time with product scenarios from your own company that you have prepared in advance.

Cross-selling

When you cross-sell, you increase the value of an order by selling the customer complementary products. When cross-selling, you should always point out a benefit to the customer. We've underlined the benefit in the examples below to show you what we mean. Cross-selling sounds like this:

You know, Nancy, many of our customers who order our "Poster Maker" software also like to get the $12.95 deluxe clip-art package. It's a <u>great value</u>, is very <u>easy to use</u>, and gives you 250 images that make your posters really <u>attractive</u>. Would you like me to send the clip-art to you along with "Poster Maker?"

To confirm, I'll send you 144 ninety-minute XR-90 cassette tapes. By the way, we're having a special on our sixty-minute XZ-60 tapes and you can <u>save 15%</u>. Do you use sixty-minute tapes?

That shirt looks fantastic on you, Mr. Zoot. Let me show you a tie that will look great with it. The nice thing about this tie is that it not only goes with this shirt, but you can also wear it with a blue or white shirt. It's very <u>versatile</u> and is a <u>good quality</u> tie at a very <u>affordable price</u>. Would you like to add it to your wardrobe?

The steps for cross-selling are as follows:

1. Make a statement to bridge from the product the customer has ordered to the product you want to cross-sell.

2. Describe the product you want to cross-sell and point out its benefits.

3. Ask the customer to buy it.

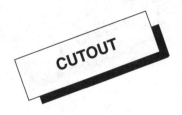

Cross-selling

Scenario One

Jermaine Montez bought two tickets for a 15-day cruise to the Virgin Islands. You know he and his wife like to scuba dive. See if they'd like to have a guided dive through the underwater park off St. John, some of the most beautiful underwater scenery available in the Caribbean. It's four hours, includes a basket lunch, and costs $150 per person.

Scenario Two

Ms. Pottsbough has just ordered a very expensive desk pad from your catalog of exclusive desk accessories. See if she is interested in the matching pen set and letter tray. The entire set just won the coveted Milano award for office furnishings and there are only 250 sets available. The pen set and letter tray retail for $685.

Scenario Three

Jimmy Rae Jones has just signed up for your weekly Mow-and-Trim lawn-care service. You know that lawns look better and are less expensive to maintain over time if your patented Weed-and-Feed solution is applied quarterly. This additional service adds $25 to the bill each month, but can save money and time in weeding and re-seeding.

Scenario Four

Mossie Smart has been shopping in your store for drapery fabric. It's clear that she is uncertain about how to make the drapes herself. You also offer sewing services, and although it would cost Mossie $400 to have the drapes made, the fabric is $700 and could easily be ruined by a cutting or sewing error.

10

What About Us?

Games for Improving Service to Your Internal Customers

You're My Customer?

In a Nutshell

This game is useful in helping participants recognize who their internal customers are. It's a simple game, but it's often a big eye-opener for participants unfamiliar with the concept of internal customers. This is a solo game in which participants complete the handouts on their own and then share their results with the group. It's ideal for employees who deal with other departments to meet customers' needs.

Time

15–20 minutes.

What You'll Need

One copy of the handout on pages 195 and 196 for each participant.

What to Do

Tell participants that they're all familiar with their external customers, but that they also have internal customers— people they serve within the organization. The customer service skills they've learned apply to their interactions with these internal customers as well.

Distribute the handouts and go over the example as a group. Then give participants ten minutes to complete their own handouts. At the end of the activity, ask for volunteers to share their findings with the group.

Tip! Offer an incentive for participants to come up with as many internal customers as they can in the allotted time.

Defining Internal Customers

Shari is a receptionist, so naturally her external customers include everyone who calls the organization and everyone who walks in the front door of the building. But she has internal customers as well. Each aspect of her job is a "service" that she provides to a "customer." By exploring her various job duties, she can define her internal customers—in this case, everyone in the organization!

Task: Answer phones
Customer: Everyone in the organization who receives outside phone calls

Task: Collect and monitor in-house visitor sheets
Customer: My boss, Terry, and the Security Department

Task: Take care of paying for lunch deliveries, and notify employees when their delivery has arrived
Customer: Different people every day—whoever orders a lunch delivery

     Now take some time to define your own internal customers. Remember that every aspect of your job ultimately serves some "customer."

Task: _____

_____

Customer: _____

Task: _____

_____

Customer: _____

Task: _____

_____

Customer: _____

Task: _____

_____

Customer: _____

Task: _____

_____

Customer: _____

Task: _____

_____

Customer: _____

Bull by the Horns

In a Nutshell

This is a brief, fast-paced game that helps participants explore and overcome the obstacles they face in delivering top-notch service to their internal customers. It also reinforces the idea that problem-solving can often be accomplished simply and quickly—just by taking the bull by the horns. It's ideal for anyone who tends to feel less inspired about internal customer service than external customer service.

Time

10 minutes.

What You'll Need

The information on page 200 copied onto an overhead or flip-chart and a watch which displays time in seconds. Participants will need pen and paper.

What to Do

Cover up all but the first question on the overhead or flip-chart. You'll reveal the questions one at a time. Before the game, ask participants to get up and stretch and take a few deep breaths to prepare themselves for some fast, energetic thinking. Remind the participants about the concept of internal customer service, and let them know that that is the focus of this activity.

Tell them that you're going to show them several questions or statements, one at a time. They should read the statement and quickly come up with at least one answer. Tell them the game moves quickly, and they'll only have seconds to come up with a response. The only rule is that they have to come up with at least one answer to each question. Each successive question relates to the answer they gave in the previous question.

Begin the activity by revealing the first question. Read the question to the class and give them the time allotted to complete their answers.

1. I could serve my internal customers better if.... (Allow 45 seconds)

2. Circle one of your answers from the previous question. (Allow 10 seconds)

3. How can you accomplish this? (Allow 45 seconds)

4. Circle one of your answers from the previous question. (Allow 10 seconds)

5. What are you willing to do to see that this gets accomplished? (Allow 60 seconds)

6. When will you do this? (Allow 30 seconds)

7. I will _____ by _____.
   action plan date

   Signed, _____
   your name

   (Allow 15 seconds)

   Ask participants to read their action plans out loud. Congratulate them for finding a solution in record time.

If You Have More Time

Play a second or even a third round to come up with more action plans for improving their internal customer service.

1.   I could serve my internal customers better if....

2.   Circle one of your answers from the previous question.

3.   How can you accomplish this?

4.   Circle one of your answers from the previous question.

5.   What are you willing to do to see that this gets accomplished?

6.   When will you do this?

7.   I will _____ by _____.
              action plan   date

      Signed by: _____

Delight Consultants

In a Nutshell

Participants work together to help one another come up with ideas to surprise, impress, and/or delight their internal customers. They benefit from the creative thinking of their peers and from the free-flowing, brainstorming tone of the game. This game works well for participants who have a number of internal customers to serve.

Time

20 minutes (longer if there are more than twelve participants).

What You'll Need

Each participant will need paper, pen, and a hard surface (such as a binder or clipboard) on which to write. A fun but optional prop for this activity is a bell or chime.

What to Do

Arrange two rows of chairs facing one another. The two rows should be close enough to allow conversation, but each chair should be separated from the ones on either side by a couple of feet.

Begin the game by asking each participant to choose one internal customer whom they would like to delight. Once they've done this, designate half the class as "clients" and the other half as "consultants" (they will switch roles halfway through the game). The clients sit in one row of chairs and the consultants in the other. During the activity, the consultants always stay seated, but the clients move down their row of chairs once every minute (when you ring the bell or tell them to move).

Each client will have one minute to ask the consultant for advice on how to delight his or her internal customer. At the end of a minute, the client moves down the row and picks the brain of the next consultant. Once every client has spoken with every consultant, tell them to switch roles and repeat the activity.

Consultants should be encouraged to think freely and offer as many ideas—no matter how outrageous—as they can to each client. This is meant to be a fun, energetic activity. The client should glean ideas from each consultant and then decide upon one course of action that will delight the internal customer.

At the end of the activity, ask for volunteers to share their plans for delighting their internal customers.

Flash!

In a Nutshell

This game is a great reminder that customer service skills can and should be applied to interactions with internal customers. This game is suitable for anyone who serves internal customers and is a nice follow-up for participants who've completed Assets and Opportunities in Chapter 2.

Time

15–20 minutes.

What You'll Need

13 large index cards and a black marker. Before the session, create the flash cards by writing one skill on each flash card.

Friendly
Efficient
Knowledgeable
Attentive
Empathetic
Honest and fair
Solution-oriented

Quick
Eager to please
Optimistic
Creatively helpful
Upbeat
Diligent

You may want to have candy or other small treats on hand for the winners or for all participants.

What to Do

Tell participants to focus on their interactions with internal customers. Tell them you'll show them a card with a customer service "asset" on it, and they have to give you an example of how they might implement that characteristic in their service to internal customers. For example, if you held up a card that said, "Poised," someone might say, "When Garth gives me feedback on my call trend sheets, I can remain poised and thank him for the input."

Divide participants into teams of two or three, and ask each team to choose a team name. As the game progresses, you can keep score on a white board or flip-chart. Teams get one point if they're the first to come up with an acceptable answer.

Flash the cards one at a time and make sure all the teams can read the cards. Start out by allowing the first team with an answer to respond to each card. If, however, one team becomes overly dominant in the game, you may want to have the teams take turns responding to the flash cards.

Discussion Questions

Q: Why is it more difficult to apply these skills to internal customer service?

Q: Is it important to provide the same level of service to our internal customers as we do to our external customers? Why?

The Gift of Gab

In a Nutshell

Participants learn to leave effective and professional voice mail messages when conveying information to their co-workers. This game is ideal for anyone who uses voice mail.

Time

15–20 minutes.

What You'll Need

An overhead or flip-chart of the information on page 208. One copy of the handout on page 209 for each group of two or three participants. Participants will need paper and pens.

What to Do

Set up the activity by briefly discussing the use of voice mail. Tell participants that they're going to be learning a technique for leaving concise, effective voice mail messages when passing along information to their co-workers.

Review the overhead as follows:

G Greeting (Greet your co-worker.)

I Identification (Identify yourself.)

F Frame the message (Give some background of why you're calling.)

T Task (State what you're asking the co-worker to do.)

I Information (Give the information your co-worker needs from you in order to carry out the task.)

N Negative option (This means the co-worker should call you back only if he or she needs more information; otherwise, you'll assume the task is carried out.)

G Goodbye (A courteous close to any message.)

Now read out the following message two times. The first time, the group should just listen; the second time, they should identify each element of GIFTING as it appears in the message. We've included the answers for you.

Hi Abe, (G) this is Jennifer in customer service (I) I just spoke with a customer who's interested in becoming a distributor for our products. She owns some stables up in Kentucky and is thinking of carrying some equipment and supplies for people who board their horses there. (F) I told her you'd give her a call to let her know how our distributorships work. (T) Her name is Jane Talbott and her number is 606/555-9872. As I said, she's in Kentucky—same time zone as us. (I) If for some reason you're not the person who would handle this, or if you need more information, give me a call at extension 274.

Otherwise, I'll just assume you're handling it. (N) Thanks, Abe. (G)

Divide the participants into groups of two or three and give each group a copy of the handout. Their task is to work within their groups to rewrite the garbled messages on the handout by using the GIFTING technique. Keep the overhead in view.

After about ten minutes, ask to hear some of the rewritten messages. Keep in mind that responses will vary, but all should follow the GIFTING model.

Explain to participants that not all messages lend themselves to this model (for example, in some situations a negative option isn't preferable, and not all messages involve a "task"), but that it's a good technique for most of their communication via voice mail.

Tip! Make a GIFTING job aid by photocopying the overhead on page 208 for participants to keep near their phones.

If You Have More Time

Have participants create their own voice mail messages based on some information they might pass along to a co-worker.

Leaving a Voice Mail Message

G   Greeting

I   Identification

F   Frame the message

T   Task

I   Information

N   Negative option

G   Goodbye

Rewrite the following voice mail messages using the GIFTING technique.

1. Hi Ron. I have a situation I'm not really sure what to do with. I think probably you're the person to handle it, but maybe not. Anyway, this guy called and he's a professor and he wants to look at some of our books for consideration in his course. I don't know what he teaches but he's at the University of Washington. He's used some of our publications before as textbooks for his courses and he said he wants a reading copy of *America's Promise, Land of the All-Too-Free*, and *Mountains Majesty*. Three books. He said he doesn't want to order them but wants, like, he'll pay if he keeps them. So can you give him a call? I wrote his number down; it's 206/555-4987. Oh yeah, his name is David Newby and that's his work number.

2. Joseph, hi. I wanted to know if I could get from you some new info sheets on two products: the Victory and the Quiet Storm. It seems I'm out of them and I talk to customers a lot about those models so I'd like to have some sheets on hand. Maybe you can just e-mail them to me. By the way, this is Eric in customer service. So if you can do all this, give me a call to let me know. I'm at extension 3276.

3. Lisa, this is Doug. I was sitting in for Daphne at the front desk today at lunch when a woman came in and gave us a checkbook she had found in our parking lot. There's no phone number on the check but the name is Ida Pinkerton and the address is 2357 Hamilton Street. I wonder if it's one of our clients. I don't have any access to our client base so Daphne suggested I give you a call to see if you might be willing to track down this woman and see if she was here and might have dropped her checkbook. Otherwise I'll call the bank. So can you please let me know as soon as possible whether you can give her a call? If I don't hear from you by 3:00 p.m., I'll go ahead and call her bank and see if they can let her know. I'm back at my desk now. You can reach me at extension 475. Thanks.

About the Authors

Peggy Carlaw is the founder and president of Impact Learning Systems International (ILSI), a training and consulting company based in California.

Vasudha Kathleen Deming works for ILSI as an instructional designer and training consultant specializing in sales, customer service, and technical support.

For more information about Impact Learning Systems International or for information on our training programs, please visit our Web site at www.impactlearning.com or give us a call at 800-545-9003.